Steam
Packet
the
album

Ferry
Publications

Stan Basnett • Miles Cowsill

IT'S THE WAY TO EXPERIENCE
'YEAR OF RAILWAYS'

The Isle of Man 'Year of Railways' has got to be one event on every enthusiast's timetable. Yet it's as close as your local station with a Rail/Sea ticket from the Isle of Man Steam Packet. Just look at these return prices to the Isle of Man - from London from £59 - from Manchester from £42.

What's more there are special Magic Holiday packages - two nights' B&B, Rail/Sea return, plus unlimited rail travel on the island from just £97. *The train leaving your local station is THE way to experience this unique event.* Phone Anne or Jane for your 1993 Sailing Guide and Magic Holidays brochure today!

EXCLUSIVE OFFER: ALL 'YEAR OF RAILWAYS' PACKAGES BOOKED WITH MAGIC HOLIDAYS WILL RECEIVE A LIMITED EDITION REPRODUCTION OF AN ORIGINAL ISLE OF MAN RAILWAYS POSTER - *A TRUE COLLECTORS ITEM!*

INTERCITY

Tel: 0345 585833 (charged at local rates from anywhere in the U.K.) or if you prefer, write to Year of Railways Information Office, P.O. Box 5, Douglas, Isle of Man.

2

Contents

Produced and designed by Ferry Publications trading as Lily Publications Ltd

PO Box 33, Ramsey, Isle of Man, British Isles, IM99 4LP

Tel: +44 (0) 1624 898446   Fax: +44 (0) 1624 898449

www.ferrypubs.co.uk e-mail: info@lilypublications.co.uk

Printed and bound by Gomer Press Ltd., Wales, UK +44 (0) 1559 362371 © Lily Publications 2012

First Published: October 2005   Second & Revised Edition: June 2012

foreword

The publication of this book marks yet another chapter in the story of a company which has defied the passage of time and which continues to thrive in an ever changing world. The Isle of Man Steam Packet Company is, to the best of our knowledge, the oldest passenger shipping company in the world still trading under its original name. Since being formed in 1830 we have, for almost 182 years, remained true to our core aim of providing a reliable 'lifeline' service between the Island and its larger neighbours Great Britain and Ireland.

Much has changed over that time. Europe has fallen into and recovered from two world wars, our vessels and crews playing a key part in the process. Post Communist Europe has fragmented into many new countries. The era of mass tourism in the late nineteenth century and early twentieth century has been and gone. Paddle steamers made of wood, then iron and latterly steel have given way to more modern vessels powered by turbines and marine diesel engines. The introduction of fast powerful lightly constructed craft made from aluminium has transformed services on shorter sea routes and represents a real alternative to air travel. Competition has raised its head on several occasions, forcing both productive and destructive change as a result.

Despite all this, and in the face of yet another cyclical economic downturn across the world, the Company, without fuss or fanfare, continues to provide the consistency and reliability needed by an Island isolated in many respects by the Irish Sea. A modern successful and diverse economy needs the certainty of transport links with its trading partners to ensure free movement of goods and services.

This well-written and carefully researched book includes for the first time a number of photographs never before published relating to the largest conversion ever attempted on a fast craft. 'Manannan' (formerly HSV-X1 Joint Venture) is the most powerful vessel ever purchased by the Company. Her conversion from a US Military fast response helicopter, troop and tank carrier to arguably one of the finest passenger vessels of her type was both a challenge and a triumph for the Company. In writing this book, the authors have been granted 'behind the scenes' access in order to be able to more accurately tell the story of the men, women and vessels that today comprise the Steam Packet Company.

Whilst proud of our past we are also passionate about our future and determined to remain an integral part of Island life. The Company has faced a number of

Mark Woodward

challenges in recent years and continues to provide all that is expected of it under the User Agreement with the Isle of Man Government. But times are changing. Demand patterns have shifted and passenger and freight requirements may change too. This means that we must now look to the future. Fundamental questions regarding the type of vessels required and the routes to be serviced are essential and crucial to continued survival and success in the years ahead.

The men and women afloat and ashore who serve the Company today remain determined to play their part in its future. We are all privileged to work for a company with such a rich history and feel a deep sense of pride and belonging.

Mark Woodward
Chief Executive Officer
February 2012

*A classic photograph of the **Ben-my-Chree** (6) turning in the outer harbour at Douglas seen from Douglas Head. The castellated structure on St Mary's Isle in the background is the Tower of Refuge built in 1833 at the instigation of Sir William Hillary founder of the Royal National Lifeboat Institution. (Miles Cowsill)*

The **Lady of Mann** [1] *photographed from the end of the Victoria Pier in September 1965 leaving with the 09.00 sailing for Liverpool with the last of the Manx Grand Prix motorcycle traffic prior to going for her annual winter lay-up. (Stan Basnett)*

1830 – 2012

Introduction

In 2005 we published 'Steam Packet 175' and during the course of the research of this book a large amount of photography was uncovered which was far more than we could include in the official history book. The decision was taken at the time by the publishers to produce a second book as a companion to the first to enable these photographs, many previously not published, to be seen by enthusiasts and the many of you who love shipping and have a particular passion for the Steam Packet.

'Steam Packet – The Album' was an overnight success and outsold the original concept within six months. We have been asked many times to republish the book and the decision was taken by us both this year to republish and update the book.

Many of the original pictures are included within the pages of this publication but a lot of new material, which we are always receiving at the office, has been included to make the book more attractive. We have added a new chapter to the final pages of the publication, looking into the future of the Steam Packet in the current environment and economic conditions.

We are grateful to Mark Woodward for his encouragement and involvement with the publication. We would also like to acknowledge all those who have been involved with the original book and the new edition and particular thanks are due to Captain Peter Corrin, Captain Jack Ronan, Michael Casey, Charlie Coole, Geoff Corkish, Albert Frost, Billy Stowell, Audrey Mansell, Arthur Laine, Alex McBride, Miranda Brennan, John Hendy, David & Dorothy Parsons, Clare Price, Brian & Shirley Martin, Ken Hassell, Joan Gelling, Eric Bird, Adrian Sweeney, Bruce Peter, Ian Collard, Gordon Hislip, Carol Basnett and Dick Clague. All other parties who have helped with the book are duly acknowledged later on.

The book is not intended to be a formal history of the Company but to give it credence in its own right it attempts through historical research and anecdotal recollection to present a broader and perhaps more personal picture of the Company and its involvement in the development of the Island over the last 182 years.

As this book is published, the Steam Packet celebrates its 182nd anniversary and still retains the accolades of one of the longest and continuous shipping companies in the British Isles. We hope that this new edition will bring back memories to many islanders and visitors and will give you a further insight into this company's operations.

Stan Basnett and Miles Cowsill
June 2012

*A beautiful day in April 1969 with the **Manx Maid** (2) berthed at the Liverpool Landing Stage with her sister ship **Ben-my-Chree** (5) in the river departing for Douglas. (Eric Bird)*

*This view of the harbour from the Fort Anne Jetty taken prior to 1930 shows the Red Pier roundhead and the fine castellated lighthouse at its extremity. The pier was only 40ft wide and became congested with cargo storage, and this was one of the reasons for the widening with the viaduct completed in 1938. The new Steam Packet cargo sheds serve the Office Berth where the **Mona** [4] is berthed. (Stan Basnett collection)*

9

CHAPTER ONE

Setting the Scene

Late in 1829 a group of Manx worthies frustrated at the unreliable communication with England successfully formed an Isle of Man Steam Packet Co. The directors included a number of distinguished local gentlemen and the High Bailiff. Against all odds and in competition with established British-based steamship companies they had their first vessel built in Scotland and it entered service in the middle of August 1830. They named their vessel *Mona's Isle* and it entered service leaving Douglas for Liverpool at twenty minutes past nine on the morning of Tuesday 17th August 1830 and this was the birth of the Isle of Man Steam Packet. We know this and the passengers' names because incredibly the original way book survives in the archive of the Manx Museum.

Douglas, because of the Island's peculiar relationship with the British Government, had become a haven for smuggling and wealthy merchants had established businesses based on 'the trade' as it was known locally. Like so many places around the British Isles Douglas had developed around the mouth of a river and although not at that time the capital of the Island it did provide a safe

This well-known and often published photograph is included to show the Circus Beach and why it is so called. It also shows Pollock Rock and its fort which together with the two-gun battery on Douglas Little Head was built to protect the harbour from invasion. It was from this rocky outcrop on which the fort stood that the low water landing pier was built. (Manx National Heritage)

dry harbour with the small fishing vessels of the time being moored in the lake and other inlets at the head of the harbour. This area is now occupied by the railway station and the Tesco superstore.

The demand for increased wharfage and deeper water inevitably meant that the harbour would migrate seaward. At Douglas the first major harbour works to be undertaken was the building of a masonry pier in 1700 known as the Tongue. At the same time limestone-faced quay walls were built on both sides of the harbour marking the beginning of the North Quay and South Quay, the alignment of which can still be determined.

This interesting early photograph is from a stereoscopic card – it shows the inner harbour at Douglas and was taken not long after the formation of the Steam Packet Co., giving an idea of how trade was at the end of the 19th century. It also shows how the advent of steam was to change things for ever. (Stan Basnett collection)

*The oldest pier within the harbour is the Tongue and ships were built there up to the 1930s. The **Lady Fry** is seen being launched sideways off the Tongue into the River Douglas. The Steam Packet used the Tongue for winter lay-up of some of its vessels as we shall see later. (Stan Basnett collection)*

The only protection afforded to the inner harbour in times of easterly gales prior to the construction of the outer breakwater was the Red Pier roundhead together with the roundhead on the Fort Anne Jetty. The Red Pier was at the time of its completion the place for local society to promenade. (Collection of the late Captain Tom Corteen)

*The lighthouse built by the Isle of Man Harbour Commissioners on Douglas Head in 1832. The Steam Packet Co. paddle steamer **Queen Victoria** is leaving Douglas some time between 1887 and 1892, after which the new lighthouse was in place. (Stan Basnett collection)*

Between 1760 and 1765 the North Quay was being extended seaward ending in a pier. Land was being reclaimed from the foreshore and the town being developed in the area of the present car park by Lord Street bus station. It is hard to realise but at this time the French and English were still at loggerheads and this was vividly brought home to the Island when a sea battle took place off Jurby Head in the North of the Island in 1750 between Commodore Elliot of the Royal Navy and Francois Thurot one of the French Navy's most brilliant captains.

The British won and Thurot was killed in the battle. He was no stranger to the Island as he had lived for ten years in Douglas engaged in the smuggling trade before returning to France! It was popularly believed that he had a grudge against George Moore who was a merchant and also Speaker of the House of Keys and was bound for the Island when intercepted by the British.

Until 1765 the responsibility for the Island's harbours lay with the Island's Government and the Duke of Athol but after the Revestment Act of 1765 the harbours had been brought under the control of the Crown and the Admiralty. The seaward end of these works ended in a pier that did provide some shelter to the harbour, but a storm in 1786 demolished 84 yards of this pier and the light on the end of it.

In September 1787 the Manx herring fleet was caught in an easterly gale off Douglas returning from fishing. When they arrived off Douglas it was dark and low water. The only guiding light had been a temporary lantern on a pole which had been blown away in the storm and further damage caused to the pier. They were unable to enter the harbour and in the ensuing chaos almost 200 boats were lost with 161 crew members reported drowned. The effect on the community was devastating. The House of Keys (the Island's parliament) blamed the disaster on the poor state of repair of the harbour due to the neglect of the British authorities and called for a full inquiry.

Looking back from the root of the new breakwater towards the inner harbour along the Approach Road, work on which had commenced in 1867. (Coode Archive)

Another view of the Approach Road after completion and illustrating that it was also becoming a place to promenade. The block-casting yard for the new works is just behind the large building in the centre of the picture. (Coode Archive)

By 1791 the only harbour light at Douglas was still a lantern on a pole which was displayed only when a ship was due or all the time during the herring fishery. The need for protection of the harbour now became a major issue and numerous pleas were made to the British Government for action. The Treasury responded by sending a skilled engineer to Douglas to report on the state of the harbour. His report stressed the need for a breakwater but his overall scheme was too expensive. The eventual outcome was the construction of the Red Pier. The foundation stone was laid by the Duke of Athol in July 1793 and it was completed by 1801 at a cost of £25,000. Built of imported dressed sandstone from Runcorn it became the promenade where it was fashionable to be seen.

It was 540 ft in length and 40ft wide with a roundhead at its seaward end. It was the first attempt at a seaward extension of the harbour, providing shelter from the north east but not from the predominantly treacherous south easterly quadrant. Berths at the pier were still tidal and it was only accessible for a couple of hours either side of high water.

At low water passengers and parcels were transferred to small boats and ferried to the pier. At extreme low water such as spring neaps passengers were carried on the backs of boatmen the last few yards to the shore or pier! Despite this and intense competition from Liverpool-based competitors, the company survived and eventually won the mail contract for conveying mails twice a week.

In response to continued pressure from the Island a

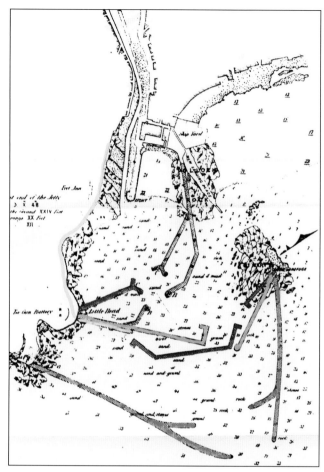

Chart showing Douglas harbour in 1847 with various proposed improvements as described in the text. (courtesy of Coode Blizard)

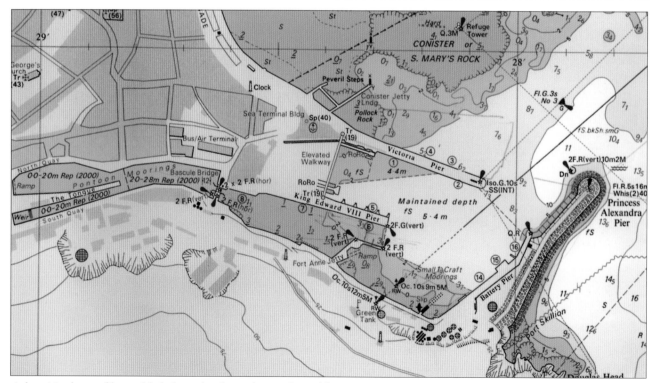

A chart giving the general layout of the harbour today, showing the inter-relation of the various piers. (Courtesy of UK Hydrographic Office)

lighthouse was constructed in 1832 by the Commissioners of Northern Lights on Douglas Head. Four years later the Fort Anne Jetty was built to a design by Sir John Rennie in an attempt to address some of the problems of the exposed position of the harbour. The wreck of the steamer *St George* on St Mary's Isle or Conister Rock as it is more popularly known gave further impetus to the plea for more protection from easterly gales at Douglas.

Now that the Isle of Man Steam Packet Company was on the scene they were able to exert more pressure on the Insular Government than many of the other off island operators. Numerous schemes were promoted over the next thirty years to provide a harbour of refuge at Douglas all of which incorporated a proposal to build a breakwater in a northerly direction from the two gun battery on Little Head at Douglas. In 1843 a detached breakwater was completed at Derbyhaven at a cost of £3,524 and the northern pier was completed at Ramsey.

Nevertheless in 1848 the House of Keys once again found the question of the general state of disrepair of the Island's harbours before them. They were of the opinion that the British Government were not discharging their obligations with regard to the maintenance and repair of the piers and harbour walls. They resolved to send a memorial to the Lords Commissioners to the Treasury and the Admiralty.

The memorial was sent on 17th December 1846 under the signature of J. T. Goldie Taubman, Speaker of the House of Keys. It is worth quoting the start of it as it gives an insight into life on the Island at this time. Remember that the Steam Packet had already been in existence for sixteen years. It also illustrated the huge gulf that existed between the haves and the have-nots!

......"That the labouring classes of the Isle of Man have heretofore subsisted upon salt herrings and potatoes, with the occasionally small quantity of oatmeal or barley meal.

That the potato crop is lost, the herring fishery of the past year has to a great extent proved a failure, and the oat crop has yielded so indifferently as to raise the price of oatmeal beyond anything known for many years.

That the distress occasioned by the circumstances above-mentioned renders it the imperative duty of thee House of Keys to lay the matter".......

It went on to plea for the improvement of the harbours throughout the Island to cater for the increased tourism and commercial business that was starting and to provide work for the labouring classes.

Despite the ever-increasing business the Steam Packet was bringing to the Island as an ideal watering hole so popular with the wealthy, they still had to land at Douglas by small boat as the harbour dried out at low water. In addition the island had no safe haven for shipping in the event of bad weather. The memorial went on to plead for additional harbour works to be carried out at all of the Island's harbours.

The matter was considered by the House of Commons and initial survey work commenced. Then in 1847 the Earl of Auckland, First Lord of the Admiralty, came to the

The photograph shows the original low-water landing pier (Victoria Pier) under construction but nearing completion, dating it at 1871. To the left is the roundhead on the Fort Anne Jetty which prior to the construction of the Battery Pier was the outer breakwater. Ships entering the inner harbour had to negotiate the entrance between it and the roundhead on the Red Pier. At low water the harbour dried out beyond this point. (Manx National Heritage)

A view of the low-water landing pier which was completed in 1872 and named the Queen Victoria Pier. The horse tramway was extended to the Peveril Hotel in 1877 and the Battery Pier breakwater was completed in 1879, so the assumption is that the photo must date from the mid-1880s. (Stan Basnett collection)

This view taken around 1905 of the extension of the Victoria Pier (as it had now become) and the infilling of the root of the pier gives some idea of the volume of holidaymakers coming to the Island at the turn of the century. (Collection of the late Captain Tom Corteen)

*In this photograph taken from a slightly different location on Douglas Head we can see the Victoria Pier extension now nearing completion, which dates it almost certainly at 1890. The **Ben-my-Chree** [2] is identified at the pier with possibly one of the Fairfield-built vessels and an unidentified North Wales Steamship vessel, and the berths on the Battery Pier are also in use. This is the photograph referred to in the text with regard to the Hercules block-setting crane. (Manx National Heritage)*

Island to view the situation. Negotiations were protracted and several schemes put forward for consideration.

The question of the protection of Douglas harbour continued to be discussed between the Island Legislature, the Admiralty and the Crown. In 1858 a Royal Commission was appointed by the House of Commons to look into the whole question of harbours in the British Isles. John Coode was the only Civil Engineer appointed to the Commission which visited thirty harbours and issued their report in 1859.

Approval was given by Tynwald (the Island's parliament made up from the House of Keys and the Legislative Council) in 1860 to the construction at Douglas of a breakwater 1,100ft long to a design by Mr Abernethy C.E. at an estimated cost of £50,000, together with one for Peel at a cost of £10,000 and one for Ramsey at a cost of £6,000.

Disagreement continued between Tynwald and the Isle of Man Harbour Commissioners who had recommended a masonry structure to the design submitted by James Walker the Admiralty engineer in similar breakwaters at Peel and Ramsey.

A contract to carry out the work was awarded to Mr Jackson of London and work commenced in 1862. During May the following year several piles gave way and Mr. Abernethy was summoned to oversee remedial work. In July Tynwald was told that "its instability had become so apparent and it was so manifestly giving way that the first severe storm would sweep it away altogether." They stopped the work with only half the projected length completed.

The breakwater which was constructed from timber frames with rubble infill was all but completely destroyed by a south easterly storm on the night of Sunday 29th January 1865. In total, 21 of the 45 timber frames were washed away completely and all but five damaged to some degree. A few days later the rest of the pier succumbed to another south easterly gale. The value of the breakwater to the harbour had been seen by all but funds for its re-construction were not forthcoming despite the efforts of Governor Loch.

Nonetheless he persevered and in March the following year he reported that the British Government were prepared to re-consider but at a cost to the Island. The deal was that the breakwater repair would go ahead subject to Tynwald providing finance. This was to be achieved by the British Government surrendering their tax revenues from the Island and allowing Tynwald to collect all revenue from the collection of duties levied on spirits and tobacco etc. The result was The Isle of Man Customs bill which effectively put paid to smuggling and led incidentally to the popular election of the Island's government for the first time.

After protracted discussion in Tynwald a decision was made to rebuild the breakwater with concrete blocks to a design by John Coode C.E. and work commenced in 1867 on the approach road to the breakwater to link with the Fort Anne Jetty and South Quay. The construction of a low-water landing pier was commenced in the same year to project seaward from Pollock Rocks, being opened by His Excellency H.B. Loch the Lieutenant Governor on 1st July 1872 and named The Queen Victoria Pier. Douglas

This superb late evening photograph full of atmosphere is taken from the Approach Road looking across at the Steam Packet cargo berth where the **Mona** *[4] is sitting dried out and unable to move for at least four hours but with a wasteful head of steam just feathering the safety valves. On the extreme right are the Imperial Buildings, the head office of the Company. (Bruce Peter collection)*

This very early photograph of Peel harbour works is included to show what an Abernethy-style breakwater looked like. Peel breakwater was constructed in a similar manner to the one at Douglas which was almost completely washed away in 1865. (Stan Basnett collection)

This is the Battery Pier block-making yard with the travelling steam gantry crane used in the manufacture of the 15-ton blocks for the construction of the Battery Pier and the Victoria Pier. The original position of the lifeboat house of the No.2 Douglas Lifeboat Station is seen through the legs of the gantry. (Stan Basnett collection)

Work in progress on what was known as the Red Pier extension scheme which was first proposed in 1908 but on which work did not start until 1929. Here the demolition of the Fort Anne Jetty roundhead is under way in 1930. (Ferry Publications Library)

The **Mona's Isle** [3] berthed at the newly-completed Victoria Pier some time between 1882 and 1887 as the pier had not yet been extended. In the foreground is the Douglas No.2 sailing and pulling lifeboat. (Manx National Heritage)

A view of the Victoria Pier Arcade showing its grand design to good effect and the glazed canopy supported on ornate cast iron columns which was added in 1905. (Stan Basnett collection)

Work in progress on the post-war widening of the Victoria Pier that included the removal of the turntable, on which the two men are standing, which was used for turning cars on the narrow pier. (Stan Basnett collection)

Westminster Dredging Co. were awarded the contract to deepen No. 4 Berth at the Victoria Pier which had silted up and was providing problems for some of the Steam Packet ships that were taking the bottom on neap tides when using this berth. (Stan Basnett)

*Work in progress with Westminster Dredging Co.'s grab dredger **WD 54** dredging the north side of the Victoria Pier in May 1970. (Stan Basnett)*

now had two non tidal berths but still no protection from easterly gales. On the same day the inaugural block for the new breakwater was laid by his wife Elizabeth. As near as can be determined a decision was made in 1876 to terminate the Battery Pier as it was now known short of its originally projected length which would have overlapped the Victoria Pier. It was completed in 1879 at a cost of £110,000. The decision was to present problems in the harbour for more than a century.

No longer did ships have to stand off at low water and anchor in the bay while passengers and mail were landed by small boat. Just as well because arrivals in 1840 were 20,000 but by 1851 had reached 48,000. Construction of the Prince's Landing Stage at Liverpool in 1857 is believed to have had a significant effect on passenger arrivals at Douglas which by 1870 had reached 100,000 per annum. At Ramsey the south breakwater was built between 1874 and 1876 but the harbour remained tidal.

At Douglas by 1879 the Manx fishing fleet comprised 400 boats of between 30 and 40 tons burden and employed about 3,000 men and boys and the holiday industry continued to grow thanks to the regular service provided by the Steam Packet vessels. Reclamation of land from the foreshore had led to the building of Loch Promenade and the construction of boarding houses to meet the demand for accommodation, many of which still exist today.

The Steam Packet now had six vessels in service – *Mona's Queen* (1), *Mona's Isle* (2), *Snaefell* (1), *Douglas* (2), *Tynwald* (2), and just in service *King Orry* (2) the longest of the vessels operated by the company thus far at 260 ft just about able to berth at the new pier. The harbour was however still exposed to easterly gales and the situation couldn't be allowed to continue. Since 1873 the Company had established regular services between Douglas and Liverpool, Fleetwood and Glasgow: with additional services between Ramsey, Liverpool and Whitehaven. By

*The powerful hydraulic excavator, which was able to work within precise limits, on the jack-up platform excavating No.1 berth. The self-propelled splitter barge **Cork Sand** which conveyed the spoil to the dumping ground off Douglas Head is moored alongside. (Stan Basnett)*

View from the bridge of **Cork Sand** *of work in progress deepening No. 1 Berth, Victoria Pier, close under the end of the Victoria Pier linkspan. (Stan Basnett)*

Laxey Towing Co.'s tug **Salisbury** *alongside the splitter barge* **Nash 5605** *and the bucket dredger* **Nash 4** *with a drilling barge moored behind working on deepening the approach channel to Douglas Harbour in connection with the new breakwater in 1981. (Stan Basnett)*

1887 a double daily service had been introduced on the Liverpool route which was to continue until 1985.

Work to extend the Victoria Pier and widen the approach to it commenced in 1887 and was completed in 1891. Douglas now had four non-tidal berths. The photograph of the *Ben-my-Chree* (2) at the Victoria Pier with the Hercules block-setting crane shows work in progress. The crane was similar to one in use at Hartlepool and had a working radius of 70 ft and a lifting capacity of 15 tons. The block-making yard was situated at the Battery Pier yard and the blocks had to be ferried to the works by steam barge.

At the same time the Victoria Pier Arcade surmounted by an elegant clock tower was completed in the centre of the triangular space enclosed at the root of the pier and in front of the Peveril Hotel. This provided the first passenger facilities at Douglas harbour with shops, barber shop, café, toilet facilities and waiting hall. In 1905 a glass-covered verandah was added to provide additional shelter for people travelling to and from the Island. Gradually covered walkways linked the two piers and travellers could at last wait for the boat under cover.

Passenger arrivals by 1913 had reached 672,919 and the pressure on the four berths raised the question again

Steam Packet car ferry **Ben-my-Chree** *[5] leaving Douglas in July 1981 and passing work in progress on the approach channel over Conister Flakes to give adequate depth for vessels on the modified approach necessitated by the new breakwater. (Stan Basnett)*

*A previously unpublished photograph of **Manxman** (2) leaving Douglas in a full easterly gale on Tuesday 16th November 1965 when she took eight hours to cross to Liverpool. It clearly illustrates the exposed nature of the harbour to easterly gales before the breakwater extension. (Stan Basnett)*

A crane driver's eye view of the job. Here a diver is being lowered in a cage to inspect the 25-ton blocks, known as stabits because of their unusual shape, to ensure that none has been displaced by the storms. (Stan Basnett)

about extending the Red Pier. The First World War intervened and the Steam Packet Company which had fifteen vessels at the outbreak of hostilities was suddenly left with four, eleven being chartered or purchased by the Government. Only four returned to resume their peacetime role *Peel Castle, Viking, King Orry* (3) and *Mona's Queen* (2). Having lost seven of its vessels and the uncertainty of the aftermath of the war no one in the Company knew how Britain would recover and whether pre-war visiting figures would be reached.

W.M. Corkill was the secretary and general manager of the company at this time and successfully steered it through the immediate post-war problems which saw it faced with the decision to sell out or carry on. He had

started with the Company in 1873 and served for fifty years having been manager since 1908. This was typical of the loyalty that existed within the Company. They need not have worried - by 1920 passenger figures had reached 606,059 and in the height of the season a maximum of 60,000 arrivals were handled in one day. Clearly more deep water berthage was a priority again.

*The winter months of 1981-82 presented problems to the contractors engaged on the new breakwater works and illustrated, if it were needed, just why the long-awaited harbour protection was proceeding. Here the **Lady of Mann** [2] leaves Douglas in the teeth of an easterly gale in January 1982 while the contractors wait to see if their work has suffered. (Stan Basnett)*

Work on placing the armour almost finished prior to completion of the infill and constructing the wave wall. The two Lima cranes were the largest the Island had seen on any construction work. (Stan Basnett)

One of the primary armour concrete stabits on the crane barge awaiting placement using the third of the large cranes used on the project. (Stan Basnett)

Consideration had been given to extending the Red Pier and providing low-water landing facilities in the period leading up to 1914. The outbreak of war put paid to progress until 1922 when the scheme was resurrected. After further modifications the scheme was approved in 1929 in its final form to a design by W.H. Blaker, Chief Engineer to the Isle of Man Harbour Commissioners.

The South Quay wall was demolished and rebuilt in concrete blocks and became the Steam Packet Co.'s dedicated cargo berth. The berthage around the extended pier was deepened beyond a 16ft high bar at the root of the new pier, the harbour landward of this was still tidal. Dredging was carried out by the James Dredging, Towage and Transport Co., Ltd of Southampton using their bucket dredger *Foremost 49*.

With access to the Pier through the South Quay and the cargo berth it was recognised that the approach to the new pier had to be by other means if 4,000 passengers were to be handled in half an hour. Viaducts were constructed over the Circus Beach which served an important function as a spilling beach, giving both vehicular and pedestrian access to the new pier from Bath Place. Provision was also made for an additional berth on the southern viaduct.

The work was completed and opened in May 1936 by the Secretary of State for the Home Department the Rt. Hon. Sir John Simon and named the King Edward VIII Pier becoming one of the few public structures to carry the abdicated King's name.

The Second World War once again intervened and the Steam Packet Company found eleven of its ships requisitioned for war service. *King Orry 3*, *Mona's Isle 4*, *Manx Maid 1*, *Mona's Queen 3*, *Viking*, *Tynwald 4*, *Fenella 2*, *Manxman 1*, *Lady of Mann 1*, *Ben-my-Chree 4* and later *Victoria*. At the end of the war the Company had lost four ships and one, the *Manxman* was in such a poor condition that it was scrapped without coming back on service.

Very little alteration took place in the harbour at Douglas other than the widening of the Victoria Pier and the removal of the double corner in 1954 in the inner harbour and the removal of silt in parts of the outer harbour until the provision in 1965 of the new passenger terminal built on the site of the old Victoria Pier Arcade. Work on its demolition started in 1961 and construction of a new waiting hall commenced. The transformation was spectacular but it had come too late really and most of its design functions never came into play. The same year saw *Mona's Queen 5* take the last sailing from Fleetwood due to the British Transport Commission declaring that the berth was in a dangerous state and beyond repair.

The unusually designed Sea Terminal had three main concourses linking the two main piers and fronting Peveril Square. The Crows Nest restaurant, soon to be christened the "lemon squeezer" was on the third floor situated below the tall central spire commanding views over the harbour and the promenade. The Terminal was completed in 1965 and formally opened by Princess Margaret.

Much of the space was very gradually given over to Government departments as offices. The waiting hall continues to serve the travelling public and the Steam Packet now operate its ticketing facility from there – a far cry from the brown wooden ticket kiosk on the pier at the foot of the gangway!

The advent of Ro-Ro services on short sea crossings was to have a great effect on the harbour and the Company which had for so long resisted the capital outlay on full roll on roll off vessels. Their decision was largely influenced by the lack of facilities at some of the ports to

*A post-war photograph of the **Ben-my-Chree [4]** and **King Orry [4]** at the Victoria Pier and in the foreground two steam cranes on the Battery Pier, by way of contrast to the size and capacity of those in use on the new works. (Stan Basnett collection)*

which they operated. Instead the Company developed a unique type of side-loading car ferry which enabled cars and vans to access the vessel at different states of the tide by means of internal ramps. Four such vessels were eventually built, two steam turbine driven followed by two passenger motor ships. The *Lady of Mann 2* was still operating in 2005 and finding useful charter work in what promised to be her last year of operation after 30 years of service to the company. Later the same year, she was sold to SAOS Ferries of Greece.

This substantial investment in side-loading car ferries was one of the reasons that the Steam Packet had not progressed with a Ro-Ro service. Reluctant to commit more capital on the provision of Ro-Ro facilities without an equal investment by Government on outer harbour protection works resulted in protracted stalemate discussion with the Insular Government over the need for a breakwater extension, an argument that had been rumbling on for years.

However the advent of a rival company Manx Line with the intention of operating a full roll on roll off service between Douglas and Heysham changed all that. An approach road was built by the IOM Harbour Board to access a linkspan serving No.1 berth on the Victoria Pier in a joint venture with the new company and Douglas had its first link span which became operational in August 1978. The harbour was still exposed to easterly gales and when such conditions prevailed vessels were diverted to Peel as the berths in the outer harbour were untenable. The Steam Packet's caution had been well founded as the new

linkspan was severely damaged in an easterly gale in December the same year.

The Steam Packet Company had no alternative now but to respond to the challenge of providing a Ro-Ro service between Douglas and Liverpool. With no help coming from Government and difficulties over reaching an agreement for the construction of a linkspan they eventually entered into an agreement to lease a portion of the harbour bed on the South side of the Edward Pier on which to site their own linkspan but subject to the condition that it could be relocated later when the latest round of harbour improvements had been completed.

A linkspan was ordered from O.V. Navire of Finland and it arrived under tow of the Finnish tug *Kraft* on 2nd June 1981. It was positioned the following day by the tugs *Salisbury* and *Union* of the Laxey Towing Co. and successfully flooded down in the position it was to occupy for the total time it was in use on the Island; apart from a short sojourn to repair damage caused by *Peveril 4* encountering a mechanical problem during berthing. This linkspan is now located at Heysham which does illustrate the versatility of its novel design.

Work on the long-awaited new breakwater designed by Sir William Halcrow and Partners and constructed by French Kier commenced in 1981. It was completed in 1983 and named by HRH Princess Alexandra on 14th July. It was constructed from 700,000 tons of granite secondary armour around a central core and clad with 4,000 concrete blocks each weighing 23 tons. At last the harbour was fully protected.

This photograph shows the work in progress on the demolition of the King Edward VIII Viaduct to make way for a new marshalling area to service the needs of the increasing RoRo traffic using the harbour from the new linkspan which was part of the 1980 harbour development plan. (Stan Basnett)

The new breakwater (The Princess Alexandra Pier) altered the approach to the entrance of Douglas harbour significantly and with deeper draft vessels coming on service it was clear that some major work would be required to ensure sufficient depth in the approach channel. The work was undertaken concurrently by Nash dredging using their drilling barge to deepen the channel over Conister Flakes to 5m below harbour datum. After the blasting was completed the bucket dredger *Nash 4* and accompanying splitter barge *Nash 5605* completed the work.

In 1985 the Company became involved in a merger with Sealink, the main effect of which was to cease its links with Liverpool thus change its principal route to the UK to Heysham and inheriting *Manx Viking* which was absorbed into the fleet. By one of those strange quirks of fate it was the *Mona's Queen 5* that took the last sailing from Liverpool on Saturday 30th March as it had done on cessation of the Fleetwood sailings. However in response to pressure sailings were re-introduced on the route during 1991 with the *Lady of Mann* [2] at weekends in the winter.

The arrival in 1990 of *King Orry [5]* necessitated some deepening at No.1 berth on the Victoria Pier which was carried out by PW dredging using a hydraulic back hoe *Skua* and the splitter barge *Cork Sand* to guarantee 5m depth at low water on the berth.

The final phase in the harbour improvements was completed between 1991 and 1994 designed by Posford Duvivier as consulting engineers and Costains as

contractors when the Circus Beach infill was completed to provide a much needed marshalling yard for the expanding Ro-Ro traffic. A new Government-owned linkspan was installed, which would at last give the harbour authorities control over the use of the berth and accordingly a user agreement was drawn up with the Steam Packet Co. Finally an overhead walkway was erected to give foot passengers access to the King Edward Pier and the improvements were complete.

The Company still retained ownership of the linkspan on the Victoria Pier which it had acquired from Manx Line when it was absorbed into the Company at the time

*As part of the plan the removal of the Steam Packet's own linkspan had to be undertaken as the lease for its location on the harbour bed had expired and here it is leaving Douglas under tow of the tug **Bramley Moore**. (Stan Basnett)*

*The floating crane **Mersey Mammoth** in the outer harbour at Douglas during May 1995 positioning the new-Government owned linkspan at the King Edward VIII Pier which was the final part of the 1980 harbour development plan. (Stan Basnett)*

of the merger with Sea Containers. Douglas did posses three linkspans for a short period until 27th March 1996 when the Edward Pier linkspan, floating once again, left under the tow of the tug *Bramley Moore*.

The final phase of the harbour improvements has been the provision of an elevated walkway to separate foot passengers walking to the Sea Terminal from traffic leaving the RoRo vessel when berthed at the Edward Pier. (Stan Basnett)

It has taken the lifetime of the Steam Packet Company to achieve the sheltered harbour so desperately fought for during the first half of the nineteenth century. Along the way it acquired the entire harbour frontage between Parade Street and Circus Beach from the small beginnings with their offices in a shop purchased from W. Blore who was a tobacconist then located in the former Imperial Hotel which the Company purchased in 1887 having bought the hotel yard and stables some seven years earlier.

In 1890 Bath Place yard was added to their holdings to provide space for their cargo warehousing and the purchase of the Royal Hotel in 1913 completed the site. The change in the manner of carrying goods from break bulk to full containerisation saw the demolition of the old Imperial Hotel and the final move to a new office built in 1969 on the site of part of the former goods and parcels offices which had been built on the site of Ohmy's Circus which the Company had acquired in 1893.

This photograph of the Company's flagship the **Mona's Queen** [3] *taken in the heady days of the 1930s demonstrates the status of the Company as the principal operator on the Irish Sea routes at the time. (J & M Clarkson collection)*

CHAPTER TWO

The Driving Force

During their 175 years the Steam Packet Company have built 46 ships for their fleet and have supplemented those as required by buying in second-hand tonnage from other operators. These vessels have come from a number of yards throughout the United Kingdom and what was generally known as Europe: with some, such as *SeaCat Isle of Man* later renamed *Snaefell*, coming from even further afield. The majority however have come from yards bordering the Irish Sea.

Because the first steam-driven paddle steamers were built on the Clyde, it is not surprising that the Company went there to John Wood & Co. for their first two vessels, with engines which were supplied on Clydeside by Robert Napier. These vessels had wooden hulls and were powered by side-lever engines of 100 nominal horsepower which were a development of the beam engines used in mines and pumping stations but adapted for marine use.

Napier had built his first side-lever engine at his works at Camlachie in 1824 and so the Steam Packet Company was an early operator of these engines. In order to keep the centre of gravity low and to reduce the height of the engines, Napier cleverly located the beam below the cylinder and the side lever enabled the straight-line movement of the piston to be transmitted to the beam without the need of a crosshead or guides. The engines operated on low-pressure steam believed to be in the region of 15 pounds per square inch (psi) and drove the paddles at 16 revolutions per minute (rpm). This was to set the pattern for the future and the Company, as we shall see, always was, and still is, at the forefront of the development of sea travel.

Robert Napier's yard built the next four ships except the hull of *King Orry* which was built at John Winram's yard in Bath Place, Douglas, towed to Scotland and fitted out on the Clyde by Robert Napier. All had side-lever engines, but only the first four had wooden hulls; the rest were built with iron hulls. For the next seven ships they stayed with Clydeside companies: J.&G. Thomson of Govan, Tod & McGregor, Meadowside, Glasgow, Caird & Co., Greenock, R. Duncan & Co. and Robert Napier.

It was to be 1860 before the Company moved away from the side-lever engine to the oscillating engine where the cylinders were mounted on trunnions directly below the crankshaft. This allowed the cylinders to swing, which enabled the piston rods to act directly on the crankshaft without the need of an intermediate crosshead and connecting rod. The paddle wheels were fixed directly to

*A set of vertical compound engines as fitted to the **Mona** [2] which were the third generation following the side-lever and oscillating engines that were ideally suited for the paddle steamers. The vertical compound represented a huge step forward in economy and for the new type of screw propulsion. (I.O.M.S.P.Co.)*

*A triple expansion engine built by Fairfield Shipbuilding & Engineering Co. and fitted to the **Tynwald** [3]; the high-pressure cylinder working at 160 psi was typical of the type of engine fitted to screw vessels at the turn of the 19th century. (I.O.M.S.P.Co.)*

*The largest paddle steamer that the Company owned was the **Empress Queen** - she was powered by two sets of diagonal triple-expansion engines operating at 140 psi on the high-pressure side and each engine produced 5,000 ihp. (I.O.M.S.P.Co.)*

*The **Viking** was the first Company vessel to be powered by steam turbines designed and built by Parsons and are within the black engine casings in this photograph of the engine room. (I.O.M.S.P.Co.)*

the ends of the crankshaft. The first such engine was installed in the *Mona's Isle* [2], built on the Clyde by Tod & McGregor. This type of engine had fewer moving parts, was easier to operate and occupied less space. After 23 years operating as a paddle steamer the vessel was converted to screw propulsion, fitted with a compound steam engine and renamed *Ellan Vannin*, continuing in service for a further 26 years before being tragically lost on passage from Ramsey to Liverpool.

The next six ships were fitted with oscillating engines and all except the *Ben-my-Chree* [2] were built on the Clyde. In 1875 the Barrow Shipbuilding Co., Barrow-in-Furness had successfully tendered for the *Ben-my-Chree* [2] which was at that time the largest vessel in the fleet. She was to be a disappointment and did not meet her design speed. Even after the fitting of additional boilers she was still considered slow. She did, however, earn the distinction of carrying four funnels after the new boilers were fitted. Despite this setback the Company continued to trade with the Barrow Company who were to build three more ships for them.

The *Mona* [2] built in 1878 was a significant departure for the Company and was the first single-screw-driven vessel built and fitted with a vertical compound engine by William Laird & Co., Birkenhead – the forerunner of Cammell Laird with whom the Company were to become synonymous. The compound engine was able to effect economies on running costs as the higher pressure steam from the new generation of boilers could be used twice - first powering the high-pressure cylinder and then being exhausted to the second low-pressure cylinder, and with the addition of surface condensers the exhaust steam could be returned to the boilers enabling fresh water to be used for steam-raising.

The next vessel *Fenella* [1] built in 1881 at Barrow was the first twin-screw vessel to be owned by the Company and one of the earliest examples of this form of propulsion, using two screws driven by two separate compound engines directly driving the propeller shafts

with the thrust transferred to the hull through thrust blocks.

The *Mona's Isle* [3] was the first steel-hulled ship and was built in 1882 by Caird & Co. at Greenock; she was yet another milestone. The boilers operated at 90 psi and the compound oscillating engine had a high-pressure cylinder with a diameter of 65 inches and a huge low-pressure cylinder with a diameter of 112 inches. The engine operated at 30 rpm, turning two 28 feet diameter paddle wheels with ten floats or paddles each 11ft 6 inches wide and 3ft 11 inches deep. The sight of the moving parts of such an engine must have been awe-inspiring to the casual observer.

Engine development was gathering momentum and the benefits of screw propulsion over the paddle occupied the minds of many engineers involved with shipping. The Fairfield Shipbuilding & Engineering Co. of Govan, however, were in no doubt that there was still a future for the paddle steamer and developed a new type of non-reciprocating engine giving an indicated horsepower (ihp)

*Whereas the **Viking** was driven by direct turbines connected to the propeller shaft, the **Lady of Mann** [1] was driven by geared turbines (seen in the photograph with the casings removed) operating at a higher engine speed, at a pressure of 220 psi and connected to the shafts by reduction gearing. (I.O.M.S.P.Co.)*

The engineers' manoeuvring platform of the **Lady of Mann** *[1] from which the engineers controlled the engines in response to instruction from the bridge by means of the telegraph situated immediately in front of them. Note the speaking tube used in the event of a breakdown of the telegraph. (Stan Basnett)*

of 6,500. They built a vessel speculatively in 1887 with the Steam Packet in mind as their prospective client.

The Company, it would seem, did not take kindly to the idea and refused to buy. Fairfields set up a rival company styled the Isle of Man, Liverpool & Manchester Steamship Co., more commonly known as Manx Line, and ran in opposition building a second vessel, their ships being patriotically named *Queen Victoria* and *Prince of Wales*. The ships were more powerful than anything that

The boiler front plate of the forward stokehold in the boiler room of the **Lady of Mann** *[1]. The boilers operated at a pressure of 220 psi which enabled the turbines to produce 11,500 shaft horsepower. (Stan Basnett)*

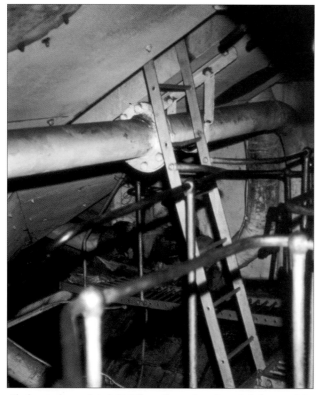

The hottest place on board ship! The walkway above the main boiler tops of the **Lady of Mann** *[1] which were double-ended, oil-fired cylindrical Scotch boilers. (Stan Basnett)*

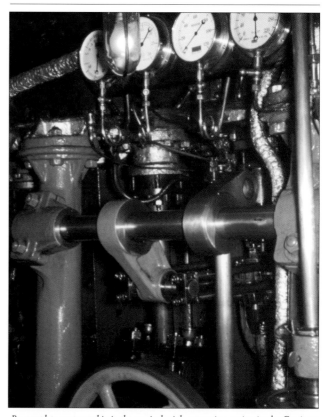

By complete contrast this is the vertical triple-expansion engine in the **Conister** *[1], generating 430 brake horsepower. (Stan Basnett)*

*The engine room of the **King Orry** [4]. An unusual feature on this ship was the floor-mounted turbine gland steam control valves essential for maintaining vacuum when slowing down. Note the space around the manoeuvring platform in this builders' photograph of a pristine engine room. (Wirral Museum Service/Cammell Laird Archive)*

*The boiler room of the **Ben-my-Chree** [5] was fitted with the integral furnace boiler; the much more spacious boiler room was due to the stabiliser equipment being more compact than that on the **Manx Maid** [2]. (Stan Basnett)*

more power from the steam by the use of an intermediate cylinder between the high and low-pressure cylinders.

Despite the apparent advantage of the screw over the paddle the Steam Packet took delivery of another paddle steamer from Fairfields in 1897. Becoming the *Empress Queen* she was fitted with two compound diagonal three-crank engines having one high-pressure cylinder and two low-pressure developing 10,000 ihp. These engines were the ultimate development of the marine steam engine that

the Steam Packet possessed and faster. The inevitable happened and the Steam Packet bought the two vessels from their rival. They must have been impressed because they had no hesitation in continuing to deal with Fairfields and in 1891 the Company ordered the *Tynwald* [3], their first triple-expansion-engined steamer with twin screws and fitted with electric lighting from new. Operating at a higher boiler pressure but having a lower ihp of 3,800, the vessel was capable of comparable speeds with the *Queen Victoria*. The triple-expansion engine was able to squeeze

*The main electrical switchboard on the **Ben-my-Chree** [5]. (Stan Basnett)*

*The engine room manoeuvring platform on the **Ben-my-Chree** [5]. (Stan Basnett)*

the driving force

The maze of dials and controls facing the engineers at the manoeuvring stand, all of which were vital when dealing with live steam. This photograph was taken on the Mona's Isle [5]. (Stan Basnett)

A close-up view of the same control stand showing the prominent position of the telegraph. Immediately above are the emergency telegraphs which strangely were used by the bridge when manoeuvring astern at Fleetwood or Belfast. The quick response of the engineer was vital to those on the bridge when operating in confined waters. (Stan Basnett)

was used for paddle steamers. The shaft driving the paddle wheels weighed 70 tons and the engines drove the paddles at the incredible speed of 44 rpm. The paddles, always referred to as floats, were of the self-feathering type, entering and leaving the water vertically with ten floats to each wheel, surprisingly only dipping in the water 10 inches despite being 11ft long and 4ft 8 inches deep.

The *Empress Queen* had four double-ended boilers with eight furnaces to each boiler and steam was raised at 140 psi. The sixteen stokers would have had very little rest! She was the largest paddle steamer operated by the Company and considered to be the most advanced paddle steamer ever built.

The vessel established a record run from the Rock Light at New Brighton to Douglas Head Light of 2 hours 57 minutes with an average speed of 23.07 knots on 13th September 1897, repeating similar timings on numerous occasions. The total timing Landing Stage to Pier was 3 hours 2 minutes! The Company acquired their last paddle

steamer, also built by Fairfield, second-hand from the Liverpool & Douglas Steamers in 1903 and named the vessel *Mona*. [3] The era of the paddle steamer had ended although the paddlers remained in service until 1929.

Perhaps the most significant development in propulsion came with the steam turbine invented by Charles A. Parsons whilst in the employment of W. G. Armstrong & Co., the famous engineering firm based in Newcastle-on-Tyne. Seeing its potential he set up his own firm to develop the idea and in 1897 built the *Turbinia* which by her dramatic intervention at the Naval Review celebrating Queen Victoria's Diamond Jubilee convinced the Admiralty that here was the means of propulsion for the future. Although more expensive to build, the efficiency of the turbine over the reciprocating engine had by 1901 convinced commercial shipping operators that they too should follow the lead of the Admiralty.

The first turbine-driven steamers were built and operated in Scottish waters, being built by William Denny

Although still a steam ship the control stand of the Ben-my-Chree [5] has become more simplified with less gauges and an increasing degree of automatic control giving the area a less cluttered feel. In the foreground left is the boiler turbo feed pump.(Stan Basnett)

The engine room of the Ben-my-Chree [5] with the double reduction gearboxes prominent in the picture behind one of the Pametrada-designed turbines in the top left of the photograph. (Stan Basnett)

*The boiler front of one of the three boilers of the **Mona's Isle** [5] showing four of the oil-fired furnaces. (Stan Basnett)*

*Engine room of the **Ben-my-Chree** [5]. (Stan Basnett)*

of Dumbarton. They also built cross-channel packet steamers for the railway companies. In 1905 the Company following these developments made their decision to build their first triple-screw turbine-driven vessel but not on the Clyde. The *Viking* was built by Armstrong Whitworth of Newcastle-on-Tyne with turbines built and installed by Parsons Marine Steam Turbine Co. This was a truly Tyneside vessel with the boilers being made by the Wallsend Slipway & Engineering Co.

The engine layout was the first of what was to become an established pattern for all the three-screw vessels with three direct-coupled ahead turbines - high pressure on the centre shaft and low pressure on the wing shafts, with two astern turbines on the outer propellers only. Reading the

records of the Superintendent Engineer C. J. Blackburn it is clear that the vessel met the Company's expectation, setting a new record from the Rock to the Head of 2 hours 53 minutes at an average speed of 23.32 knots on 3rd July 1906. On trials the six-hour continuous timing had registered 23.53 knots. Almost to prove that it was no freak, another record was set the following May: Douglas Head to the Lune Buoy in 2 hours 3 minutes, the average speed being 24 knots. The engine room temperature was recorded at 108° Fahrenheit!

This speed was obviously not achieved without some cost as the Chief Engineer J.R. Kelly (later to become Superintendent Engineer) and Captain Keig in September the following year carried out vibration tests in the main saloons and the shelter deck aft. The first was carried out with all three engines running and then with just the two low-pressure turbines driving the outer screws only and the centre engine stopped. It was noted that the vibration was much reduced on two engines but the speed was reduced to 19.7 knots. Amongst other interesting

Another view of one of the Pametrada turbines and gearboxes showing the compact nature of the machinery which produced 4750hp. (Stan Basnett)

*Engine room of the **Lady of Mann** [2] showing one of the 12-cylinder Pielstick engines manufactured under licence by Crossley. (Stan Basnett)*

the driving force

Above: *Not Dante's Inferno but the stokehold of the* **Viking** *which had four double-ended boilers with twenty-four furnaces and we know from the engineers' reports that temperatures of 108°F were regularly recorded. The* **Viking** *carried a crew of ninety and almost half were engineers and engine room ratings. Engineering apprentices were often carried as engineers on the ships in the summer and the crewing lists show that the* **Viking** *carried a seventh engineer and on average twenty-two stokers. Average coal consumption on a normal Douglas to Liverpool sailing was 33 tons. (Peter Kelly collection)*

Right: *The boiler room of the* **Manx Maid** *[2] showing the Babcock & Wilcox integral furnace boilers which were a departure from the sectional header type used hitherto. Contrast this with the conditions above which clearly illustrate four decades of development of the steam turbine-driven ship. (Wirral Museum Service/Cammell Laird Archive)*

*The **Rapide** arrives from Belfast during the TT Festival in 2004 whilst the **Lady of Mann** (2) loads pending her evening sailing to Heysham. (Miles C...*

*Close-up of one of the two engines in the **Lady of Mann** [2] showing the 'V' formation of the cylinder block. (Stan Basnett)*

*The starboard propeller shaft of the **Lady of Mann** [2] showing the tailshaft bearing and the KaMeWa oil distribution system. (Stan Basnett)*

experiments carried out on the *Viking* was one to observe the effect of a full complement of passengers gathering on one side of the ship to disembark. It was found that the angle of heel was 10° which had the effect of dropping the deck 4 feet from normal trim, a factor to be taken into account by the Master on selecting the berth at the pier.

The Company, satisfied that the new type of propulsion was the winning formula, ordered another triple-screw turbine steamer to run on the Liverpool route as a running mate to the *Viking*, now firmly established on the Fleetwood station. The *Ben-my-Chree* [3] was built by Vickers Sons & Maxim of Barrow and the vessel achieved an average speed of 23.84 knots over the measured mile on the Clyde. It is recorded that this was achieved without cleaning the fires!

The six-hour trial over the course between Cumbrae and Skulmartin Lightship, a distance of 73.7 nautical miles at full speed, recorded an average speed of 24.56 knots. The fastest speed achieved was on the return leg between

Skulmartin and Corsewall - a distance of just over 29 nautical miles when an average speed of 26.54 knots was recorded but with the tide. The Steam Packet were well satisfied with their new ship. She became the fastest ship operated by the Company until the advent of the new generation of fast craft. The record between Rock Light and Douglas Light was broken on 6th June 1909 with a time of 2 hours 48 minutes - an average speed of 24.01 knots.

The *Snaefell* [3] was the next ship the Company had built and she was a complete contrast, but of note because she was the first vessel to use 4-cylinder vertical triple-expansion engines. Designed as a cargo and passenger ship principally with economy and winter service in mind, she was a twin-screw vessel with a service speed of 19 knots.

The Company increased their fleet with second-hand tonnage until 1927 with the noted exception of the *King Orry* [3,] built and engined in 1913 by Cammell Laird. She was a twin-screw ship and the first of the Company's

*The **Mona's Isle** [6] was fitted with four main engines in a 'father and son' arrangement, two 12-cylinder and two 6-cylinder engines manufactured by M.A.N. and joined to the gearbox by independent clutches. This is the port 12-cylinder engine. (Stan Basnett)*

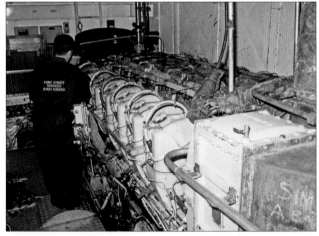

*The intensive schedule of the fastcraft and having un-manned engine rooms on passage means essential maintenance can only be done during any available lay over time. Here engineers work on one of the Ruston main engines of **SeaCat Isle of Man** overnight at Douglas. (Stan Basnett)*

*The port propeller shaft on the **Mona's Isle** [6] showing the shaft bearings and illustrating the greater room available in the shaft tunnel space compared with the photograph of the shafting arrangement on the **Lady of Mann** [2]. (Stan Basnett)*

*The control room on the **Ben-my-Chree** [6] showing again how things have changed. No longer are the engineers required to control the engines while manoeuvring as the ship is under the direct control of the bridge through her variable pitch propellers. (Stan Basnett)*

vessels to be powered by geared turbines, all the previous turbine-driven ships being driven directly off the shaft of the turbine. The single-reduction turbines gave a lower propeller speed making them more efficient. The Company had carried out numerous trials with their own vessels to determine whether three-bladed or four-bladed propellers were more efficient, measuring the amount of slip and observing cavitation which is a problem encountered with high propeller revolutions.

The first new build for fourteen years was launched from Cammell Laird in 1927: *Ben-my-Chree* [4], the first of three similar ships. The *Lady of Mann* [1] was built in 1930 by Vickers Armstrong in Barrow and the *Mona's Queen* [3] in 1934 also by Cammell Laird. In many ways they represented the ultimate development of the cross-channel steam packet ship. Their internal fittings, stairways, saloons and dining rooms were by the standards of the day sumptuous and for the holidaymakers from the industrial north must have been the equivalent of the

modern cruise vessels of today.

The *Cushag* was the first cargo-only ship owned by the Company and was bought second-hand in 1920 for trade to the Island's other ports. She and the *Conister* were single-screw, single-hatch steam coasters typical of the period and driven by vertical triple-expansion engines. The first cargo vessel specifically designed for the Company was the *Peveril* [2] built by Cammell Laird and driven by a direct-coupled triple-expansion engine.

The building in 1936 of the *Fenella* [2] and *Tynwald* [4] by Vickers Armstrong at Barrow specifically for all-year-round working heralded a new era in the ships of the Company which was to be interrupted by the Second World War. The vessels entered service in 1937, having a hull form developed from years of experience and the first with a cruiser stern and a draught and length ideally suited for Douglas Harbour. They were equipped with water-tube boilers operating at 250 psi, which had been pioneered in the *Mona's Queen* [3]. They were not to

*One of the two MAK 9M32 main engines of the **Ben-my-Chree** [6]. Each is rated at 4,500kW at a crankshaft speed of 510 rpm. The engines are subject to less stress as they operate at a constant speed whilst under way and manoeuvring. (Stan Basnett)*

*A view along the top of the same engine showing its compact nature compared to the engines in the **Mona's Isle** [6]. Virtually all monitoring of the engines is by computer and the Duty Engineer is able to control everything whilst seated at a desk in the control room. (Stan Basnett)*

the driving force

*The oil separators in the engine room of the **Ben-my-Chree** [6]. (Stan Basnett)*

survive the Second World War but their design survived, setting the pattern for the post-war all-year-round passenger ships.

The *King Orry* [4] was the first of five ships built from 1946 after the war by Cammell Laird and based on the pre-war design. They were efficient, quick and economical. The *Manxman* [2] was the last of the genre and represented the final development of the steam-turbine-powered ships, being equipped with two Pametrada turbines and operating on superheated steam at 350 psi. The turbine rotor shaft speed was an incredible 4,300 rpm and the propeller shafts were driven through a double-reduction gearbox to give a propeller speed of 270 rpm. Similar power plants were installed in the side-loading car ferries *Manx Maid* [2] and *Ben-my-Chree* [5].

The *Fenella* [3] was the first modern cargo vessel built by the Company and the first motor ship. She was powered by a 7-cylinder British Polar engine. Although three more steam-powered vessels were to be built after her, she was to signal a change and the end of the steam era, and two more motor cargo ships *Peveril* [3] and *Ramsey* were built at Troon before the twin-screw steam-turbine-powered vessel *Ben-my-Chree* [5] became the last steam-driven ship to be operated by the Company.

All subsequent vessels were powered by diesel engines. The first passenger vessel was the car ferry *Mona's Queen* [5] built by the Ailsa Shipbuilding Company at Troon in 1972 and fitted with two 10-cylinder Crossley Pielstick engines of 10,000 hp. To maintain her design speed of 21 knots these engines ran at 520 rpm, were highly loaded and as a consequence were costly on maintenance. The second diesel passenger vessel *Lady of Mann* [2] built at the same yard was fitted with more powerful 12-cylinder engines in the light of experience gained in operation with the *Mona's Queen* and were de-rated to maintain 21 knots at 465 rpm. They both had controllable-pitch propellers

and stabilisers and had bow thrust propellers making them extremely manoeuvrable. The use of bow thrusters was considered to be such a huge step forward - facilitating the ability of the ships to berth in confined spaces such as Douglas Harbour particularly when windage was a factor - that steam-powered bow thrusters were retro-fitted to the two steam-powered car ferries. This was the first time that steam-powered bow thrusters had been fitted to any vessel and it attracted the interest of the Admiralty to observe them in operation.

A number of different second-hand motor-driven passenger ships were acquired by the Company with a variety of engines, with no standard make other than they were all diesel engines. The engineers may have had a different view! The engine layout in the *Mona's Isle* [6] was unusual having four M.A.N. engines in a 'father and son' arrangement with one 12-cylinder engine coupled in line with a 6-cylinder engine to each propeller shaft.

The first aluminium-hulled vessel *SeaCat Isle of Man* was acquired in 1994 and represented a quantum leap forward in sea travel on routes operated by the Company. She was three years old when she joined the fleet and was the first fast craft to be operated by them. The vessel is a catamaran type and the two slender wave-piercing hulls are fabricated from welded aluminium - these accommodate fuel and water tanks as well as the engines, each section compartmented by watertight bulkheads. The vessel is driven by four Lips LJ135DLX water-jets which are configured for steering and reverse. These are directly coupled to four Ruston 16RK270 sixteen-cylinder diesel engines of 4,050kW and give a service speed of 37 knots. At sea the engine rooms are not manned; engine performance is monitored and controlled by the Duty Engineer from a position to the left of the Captain on the bridge. All ancillary generating equipment and air-conditioning plant are cleverly installed to save space, even to the extent of using the roof of the main cabin which was built as a separate module and was joined to the hulls on completion prior to final fitting-out.

The *Ben-my-Chree* [6] is the latest of the line and the largest vessel ever owned by the company with a length of 124.90 metres overall and a breadth of 23.90m, almost the largest vessel that it is possible to operate in Douglas Harbour and close to the maximum for Heysham. The extra height of the ship, the first with five decks, presents more windage when turning in the confined limits of these harbours than anything previously operated by the Company. The twin LIPS CP bow thrusters soon proved their worth.

The keel of the ship was laid on 28th October 1997 and she was launched on 4th April 1998, having been built completely under cover at the yard of van der Giessen-de Noord in Rotterdam. Fitted with two MAK 9M32 engines rated at 4,500 kW she has a service speed of 19 knots and is propelled by four-bladed propellers of 4 metres in diameter. The engine room is the largest of any vessel owned by the Company and a complete contrast to those

*The day is Saturday 4th April 1998 just prior to the launch of Yard No.971, now about to be named **Ben-my-Chree** [6] in the erecting shed of van der Giessen-de Noord at Rotterdam where she was built under cover. (Courtesy of Mrs Joan Gelling)*

*The **Ben-my-Chree** [6] proceeding out of the New Waterway, Rotterdam on her way to sea trials off the Hook of Holland. This aerial view gives a good impression of her length at 124.90m overall and her breadth at 23.90m, making her by far the largest ship ever owned by the Company. (Courtesy of Mrs Joan Gelling)*

The **Ben-my-Chree** [6] sports her 175 livery as she arrives at Douglas on one of her regular sailings from the Lancashire port of Heysham. The vessel has offered an extremely reliable service to the Island since her introduction in 1998. (Miles Cowsill)

*The **Ben-my-Chree** [6] undergoing acceptance trials when it is seen whether the ship meets the design specification. The trials are also an opportunity to determine the operating parameters for future use in service. (FotoFlite)*

The **Commodore Clipper**, the near sister to the **Ben-my-Chree**, outward bound from Portsmouth on her morning sailing to the Channel Islands. (Miles Cowsill)

The **Hoverspeed France** under construction at Incat's yard in Hobart. This 74m craft was to become **Seacat Isle of Man** spending most of her career in Manx Waters. (Justin Merrigan)

of the *SeaCat Isle of Man* where conditions are very restricted and hostile with high temperatures due to the cramped nature of the installation.

It is interesting to reflect how the development of ship propulsion has advanced when reading the reports of the considerable number of experiments undertaken by some of the early engineering superintendents, comparing the performance of three-and four-bladed propellers or single, double or triple screws against paddles. I wonder what they would have thought about water-jet propulsion!

The **SuperSeaCat Two** being towed out from her builders. Built by Fincantieri in Italy she does display Italian flair in her design which more closely resembles that of a ship. She is a single-hull vessel, 100 metres overall with a beam of 17.1m, and unlike the wave-piercing fast craft behaves more in the manner of a power boat and has an operational speed of between 32 and 35 knots depending on weather conditions. (Ferry Publications Library)

the winter lay-up

CHAPTER THREE

The Winter Lay-Up

At the height of their halcyon days the Company operated as many as fifteen ships in the season to meet the demand from northern holidaymakers. This contrasted sharply with the very much reduced winter demand which was handled usually by two vessels and, when Ramsey was a regular point of departure, three. The ships were maintained whilst in service by a superb engineering staff never seen by the public other than the occasional chap in white overalls wielding a spanner to fix most likely a blocked toilet, some problem with a capstan or windlass or even a problem in the galley. Whatever their mission the ship would go nowhere if it were not for them.

This was the pattern perpetuated after the Second World War when as many as eight vessels operated the summer schedule with two on the winter service.

What then of the ships not required in the winter? Well, it became established practice to lay them up and essential repairs and maintenance would be carried out. Boilers and engines needed periodic inspection and cleaning to maintain efficiency and this would be carried out in rotation under the supervision of the engineering superintendent in conjunction with the regular engineers and engine room crew of the respective vessels.

These winter lay-ups were located at various ports in the UK: Glasgow, Barrow, Birkenhead and Douglas where vessels were laid up at the Tongue in the inner harbour. Latterly the *Mona's Queen* (5) and *Lady of Mann* (2) would dry-dock at Manchester due to the proximity of the

Crossley engineering works. What was life like on board, you may well ask? By modern standards pretty primitive but if you ask anyone who has been involved they will tell you many tales sprinkled liberally with humour despite the privation. Unless the crew member involved lived nearby all staff lived on board but not necessarily in their crew quarters.

On arrival at the port where the vessel was to be laid up for the winter the deck crew would remove all the equipment out of the lifeboats and take all the lifebelts from their deck lockers and store them below. All the hemp ropes not in use would similarly be stowed and layered on the shelter deck under cover to allow the air to circulate and prevent rot. As the later polypropylene ropes came into use there was less need to store the ropes.

Covers would be put on ventilators and telegraphs and caps on funnels. Once that was complete, usually about a fortnight's work, the deck crew would be paid off and not be required again until the preparations for the following season. The crew would invariably find themselves out of work for the winter months. Many would sign on as Able Seamen on either coasters or deep sea vessels for a short term. If they returned back home to the Island in the

*The winter lay-up was also an opportunity for vessels to undergo essential maintenance which in the early days occupied considerable time. Here is a wonderful photograph of the paddle steamer the **Prince of Wales** in dry dock. (Ferry Publications Library)*

*This view of Douglas Harbour is included to show how the inner harbour at Douglas has changed. The **Douglas** [2] is laid up at the Tongue for the winter amongst the summer pleasure boats and the topsail schooners at the North Quay engaged on the cargo trade to the Island. (Stan Basnett collection)*

*The smoke is from Clinch's Brewery on the North Quay. The **Mona's Queen** [2] and **Tynwald** [3] laid up at the Tongue for the winter. The funnels are capped and we can see why the concrete fenders were built to stop the paddle boxes fouling the quay wall on the falling tide. (Bruce Peter collection)*

immediate post-war period they would be faced with the possibility of relief work on the winter vessels, the dole or the peculiarly Manx Winter Work Schemes devised by the Island Government to relieve unemployment in the winter months.

For the engineering staff though the lay-up time was totally different. It was a time when essential maintenance could be carried out. Boilers had to be washed out and de-scaled, bilges cleaned and inspected and tanks cleaned. This work was carried out by the engineering ratings, mainly stokers. The job was notoriously dirty and they were always referred to as the 'black gang'. In later years this atrocious work was carried out by sub-contractors who incidentally inherited the title!

The engineers meanwhile would set about opening up the engines as required for survey and on the instruction of the Chief Engineer. Turbines were generally opened up every two years for inspection and any damage, usually corrosion of the blades from saturated steam, would be repaired by specialists. In the case of the reciprocating engines and later motor ships the work was generally carried out by the ships' engineers with parts provided as required from their own engineering workshops.

Fitters and apprentices from the Company's workshop would be sent to the ships to remove all the boiler fittings and valves, which would be cleaned and re-seated prior to refitting. They would be accommodated in various locations on board ship, sometimes in the after lounge with an area curtained off or on the later vessels passenger cabins would be used, particularly for those there for the whole winter.

*The **Viking** in dry dock at a so far unidentified location, but most probably Barrow which was the usual port at which the vessel was laid up between the last week in September and the middle of May every year. (Ferry Publications Library)*

*Another view of the **Mona's Queen** [2] and **Tynwald** [3] laid up at the Tongue, this time taken from the North Quay. (Bruce Peter collection)*

Engineering work would be required on all the vessels in varying degree and some of the vessels would require dry-docking for maintenance work on the propellers, rudders or even for hull painting. If propeller shafts required withdrawing for any reason which might involve renewing the white metal bearings on the thrust collars, not only would the propeller be removed but the rudder might require removal first. This has been the pattern up to the present day although the modern motor vessels tend to have longer intervals between major works.

Steam Packet crews were particularly loyal to a ship and would await the letter from the Mate in January summoning them to Barrow or wherever to prepare the ship either for Easter if they were to be the first ship out or February if they were to prepare for TT week which was always the season opener when the Island would not just wake out of its slumber but would emerge in a frenzy of activity, people and noise.

The deck crew would arrive and prepare the ship for the season, painting ship and fettling deck fittings. Painting the mast was the least popular job and usually the domain of the younger men who were hauled up the mast in a bosun's chair. Whilst it would be tolerably warm on deck it was usually cold and exposed up the mast which projected well beyond the shelter of the dock walls. The paint would also be thick and almost impossible to apply, the dodge being to put the paint pot in a pail of hot water with the dual purpose of keeping the paint soft and also preventing drips blowing off the brush as it was taken out

*This photograph taken by an unknown photographer would have entailed climbing the foremast of the **Victoria**. It is included to give another view of the covers in place on the funnels to stop rain penetrating to the boilers during lay-up. (Stan Basnett collection)*

An interesting winter view between 1946 and 1948 in Douglas Harbour with the **Victoria** *at the Tongue. On the North Quay is the* **Glen Strathallan** *and the Harbour Board workboat* **Sirdar** *is at the head of the harbour. (Stan Basnett collection)*

of the pot! The worst that could happen would be to drop the paint, the resulting mess making the culprit the most unpopular person for days.

All the equipment which had been in store was put back in place and the ship generally prepared for sea. The crew, however, at this stage were not signed on as crew but employed on the basis of casual shore labour, not signing Articles and onto full seaman's rate until just prior to sailing. The conditions of employment were Merchant Navy Home Trade with a supplemental local working agreement. The normal signing was for six months after which discharge books would be completed or new Articles signed.

During this time twelve deck ratings had to live in a dead ship in their quarters which were cold and dark. Generators were shut down at 5 p.m. until 8 a.m. and any light thereafter was from paraffin lamps - on the old steamers conditions would have been even worse. Sleeping in the bunks was difficult as condensation would run down the steel plates and it was difficult to keep dry, let alone warm. It was not unknown for the condensation to freeze on the ship laid up at Barrow and even the water in the dock to freeze at Glasgow! In the earlier vessels conditions were such that crew members had to provide their own bedding! Talking with men who lived in those conditions, they had good humour and camaraderie

judging from the anecdotes, which for the most part cannot be repeated!

Shore-based staff from the Company would be despatched to the vessel to carry out more specialist work such as the sign-writing required throughout the ship for fire points, emergency exits and bulkheads identified

The **Mona's Isle** *[5] in dry dock at Cammell Laird showing the lines developed from the pre-war* **Fenella** *and* **Tynwald** *which include a cruiser stern and other features which were perpetuated up to the last steam-powered car ferries. (Alex McBride collection)*

the winter lay-up

*This view is of the **Mona's Isle** [5] in dry dock, further illustrating the elegant lineage of this class of vessel built by Cammell Laird with the pitch of the inward-turning propellers evident. (Alex McBride collection)*

*Another view of the **Mona's Isle** [5] in dry dock this time from the bow and showing the fine lines forward and the bow rudder with which Steam Packet vessels were fitted to assist in astern navigation. (Alex McBride collection)*

where signage had been obliterated during the general repainting of the ship. The upholsterer might be required to repair seating and refit curtains which may have required repair by the seamstress at Royal Buildings.

Although there was a separate galley for the crew there was no crew cook until the 1970s and food was provided much as was the custom on coasters where the crew had a kitty and one member was designated to cook meals on the one range in the crew's quarters. Hot water for washing was also from an urn on this stove.

One of the problems associated with the lack of facilities, however, was the attraction of the pub for warmth, food and socialising which had the down-side of becoming the downfall of some. At Birkenhead, for example, one of the weekend treats was to walk to the public baths where for sixpence you could at least have a decent wash. 'Lend me a pound 'til TT week' was an often-heard plea because once sailing started the crew went

from rags to riches, earning twice and more per week than they had been earning all winter.

Conditions generally improved from 1970. Generators were allowed to run until midnight and in Douglas shore connections were made to the public electricity supply. The single room mess areas were divided up, giving more privacy to the individual watches although engineering ratings still remained separate while using common facilities for cooking, which was changed when crew's cooks were employed.

Once at sea the deck crew fell into their normal pattern of work. The crew were divided into two watches, six in the forward watch and six in the aft watch. Usually the for'd watch worked the Douglas to Liverpool run and the aft watch the return leg to the Island. The lamp-trimmer/Bosun and the main deck man together with two night watchmen (one from each watch) did not carry out watch duty which left four men on each watch to act as

A young Alex McBride standing under one of the propellers giving scale to their size. You can also see the blocks on which the ship stands, the placing of which is crucial before the water is drained from the dock. (Alex McBride collection)

*Here the painters are repainting the name and emblem on the stern of the **Mona's Queen** [5], one of the final painting tasks undertaken in dry dock where the main task would be to paint the underwater hull. (Alex McBride collection)*

*The **Manx Maid** [2] in dry dock at Birkenhead receiving repairs to shell plating in the bow section. (Alex McBride collection)*

*Stern view of the **Manx Maid** [2] showing how the wider stern of the car ferries changed, although the rest of the hull form still bears the family resemblance. (Alex McBride collection)*

helmsman and lookout, taking turn and turn about. The other two would carry out deck patrol and standby outside the crew's quarters aft. They would change duties with the other two half-way across.

On approaching port and in the case of Liverpool passing the Bar Light all hands from both watches would stand to ready for working the capstan, ropes and heaving lines as required for berthing. The Mate would be in charge on the fo'csle head with the Bosun. One AB aft would be designated in charge for which he would receive a plus rate above his normal pay; he was referred to as 'Captain aft!' The off-duty watch would be lucky to get three hours' sleep at busy periods when the ships ran

*Another view of the **Manx Maid** [2], this time the other end showing the bow thruster fitted after the experience gained with the motor ships which had them from new. The steam-turbine-driven bow thrusters fitted to both the **Manx Maid** [2] and the **Ben-my-Chree** [5] were unique to the Company. The bow rudder remained in place but was used infrequently. (Alex McBride collection)*

almost continuously.

Stewards, cooks and other staff would not join the ship until Articles were being signed, usually two or three days before sailing. There was a tremendous amount of loyalty amongst the deck crews both to the Company and particular ships and this was the case until comparatively recent times. Many of the old hands had a vast experience to draw on, some having served during wartime in Royal Navy patrol vessels - particularly armed trawlers - which saw service in extreme weather in northern latitudes. They had in many cases come from local fishing boats and the coasting trade, having started in the Ramsey Steamship Company.

As time progressed a system of training was introduced and Able Seamen had to undergo some form of basic training leading to qualifying as an Efficient Deck Hand and then progressing to obtaining a lifeboat ticket, which was a prerequisite before getting a position on a passenger vessel. Most of this initial training was undertaken on the training ship *Vindicatrix* where the initial choice was between pursuing a career on deck or in catering. Others got a chance to sign on, having worked on the boats in the summer as buffet boys or paper lads selling newspapers which was the very bottom of the ladder.

Then the annual routine would commence with as many as twenty-four sailings between the Island and Liverpool being made at the weekends. Not all the ratings were employed on a casual basis because the cargo ships ran their regular service every week through the year. They

*The **Ben-my-Chree** [5] laid up at Birkenhead in Vittoria Dock with the painter's stage alongside and the short-lived 'wiggly logo' just completed. (Alex McBride collection)*

*The two sisters lying in Birkenhead Vittoria Dock with the **Ben-my-Chree** [5] on the inside and the **Manx Maid** [2] outside, both moored dead ship. (Alex McBride collection)*

*The **Lady of Mann** [2] in dry dock for annual major survey and to have work done on the shell plating in way of the propeller tunnels – an area prone to problems with cavitation. (Alex McBride collection)*

*The **Lady of Mann** [2] again but this time a bow shot and showing the bow rudder being inspected. The bow rudders were used in navigating astern as the bow thrusters were ineffective under way. (Alex McBride collection)*

were in regular full-time employment as were the crews on the winter passenger boats and there were a number of personnel who carried out relief duty to cover for holidays. The same applied to the officers both above and below decks.

In 1887 the Company purchased the Imperial Hotel and the engineering workshop was located in what had been the stables at the rear of the hotel. The 1865 Ordnance Survey plans of Douglas intriguingly show Parade Iron Foundry fronting onto Parade Street but it is not clear if it was owned at that time by the Steam Packet Company. What is certain is that some time after that the engineering section moved across the road, accessing the rear of what had become Imperial Buildings to occupy premises later to become part of the parcels sheds.

The Steam Packet eventually bought the whole block including the Royal Hotel in 1913 in which they located their catering section, upholsterers, signwriters and sailmakers. In 1948 the workshop moved to Fort Street with the engineering department, stores and the other trades from Royal Buildings. In 1997 Fort Street

Engineering as it had now become moved to a site on the South Quay Industrial Site. The number of trades employed is now considerably less than in the earlier days. A list of the trades is appended at the end of this section with a brief description of the work they undertook.

Alan Helm, Albert Hannay and Geoffrey Makin of the Fort Street Engineering staff. (I.O.M.S.P.Co.)

*A crew member cleans the protective grease off the triple-chime whistles on the funnel of the **Mona's Isle** [5] prior to her entering the summer service. (Alex McBride collection)*

The wiggly logo was not popular and many thought it was insignificant. The next logo was more utilitarian and larger and here it is being filled in after being laid out by the painter. (Alex McBride collection)

The sailmaker and rigger David Quillan repairing a rope ladder in the warehouse yard. (Alex McBride collection)

Engineer: many were apprenticed with the Company which was valued highly within the Island and seen as a stepping stone to becoming a ticketed engineer. It was a natural progression for young apprentices on completing their training to go to sea and continue their training.

Draughtsman: preparing drawings for moulders and other trades.

Pattern Maker: self-explanatory and gradually dropped as a separate trade, the work being undertaken by the joiners as their work reduced.

Joiner: in the early days of the Company they were responsible for maintaining saloon and engine room skylights and repair of internal fittings. With the use of plastics and other modern finishings their work reduced.

Moulder: a self-explanatory trade and the Company did all its own non-ferrous casting in their own foundry with the engineers doing the necessary finishing work.

Coppersmith: responsible for fabricating copper steam pipes and deck steam pipes needed for maintenance and repair.

Tinsmith: responsible for fabricating oil lamps, oil cans for the engine room and cooking utensils.

Blacksmith: responsible for fabricating all cargo handling gear, chains, lifting hooks etc.

Boilermaker: in the early days the boilermakers had as many as thirty boilers which required attention and repair to maintain the vessels in service, and although the nature of their work changed they were still carrying out maintenance work on boilers to the end of steam.

Fitter/welder: self-explanatory and the work might embrace anything from engine room to deck fittings.

Plumber: self-explanatory and probably the least attractive job of all, being responsible for the repair of shipboard toilet facilities.

Sailmaker: once again in the early days the sailmaker had an important function making and repairing sails as all the early ships carried sails. Once again this trade changed over the years to the making of canvas lifeboat covers, covers for ventilators and telegraphs etc. In latter years this section was employed fabricating lifting slings and strops.

Upholsterer: self-explanatory - not only responsible for seating but also curtains and cabin furnishings.

Seamstress: worked with the sailmaker and upholsterer and was still employed part-time in the 1970s.

A general view of the present workshop of Fort Street Engineering – the engineering arm of the Steam Packet Co. (Stan Basnett)

Here all hands are turned to from the Engineering Department to rig the 28-ton Butters crane which was such an important element in the interim Lift On-Lift Off service. (Alex McBride collection)

The workshop is fully equipped to tackle major items as well and is called on to straighten and manufacture shafting, often at short notice. It is not uncommon for fitters to work on board on overnight sailings. Here Stewart Harland sets up one of the lathes in the workshop. (Stan Basnett)

The human face of the unsung heroes. Bob Dogherty is repairing one of the many small engineering items which are needed to keep the ships on the move. (Stan Basnett)

Signwriter: responsible for all the signs on board ship, marking amongst others fire points, assembly points and emergency instructions. It included the destination boards which were hung on the bridge wing prior to departure and signage within the Company buildings. Now this trade is virtually redundant, being replaced by standardised proprietary signs produced under health and safety legislation.

Superintendent Engineers

William Lewin &

C. J. Blackburn	June 1895 to 31st December 1921
J. R. Kelly	1st January 1922 to 19th April 1937
R. B. Moore	20th April 1937 to 31st December 1945
T. W. Craine	1st January 1946 to 1st November 1958
C. J. Kenna	2nd November 1958 to 31st March 1968
J. W. Craine	1st April 1968 to 29th December 1974

Appointed as Superintendent Engineer then redesignated Fleet Engineer

R. M. Casey	30th December 1974 to 28th June 1996

Appointed as Fleet Engineer then redesignated Technical Manager

B. Johnson	29th June 1996 to 1st July 2003

Technical Manager

F. O'Neil	2nd July 2003 to date

the winter lay-up

Top: *Two stages in casting in the Mould Shop where many brass and non-ferrous items were cast in-house when the engineering section was located at Fort Street. (I.O.M.S.P.Co.)*

Middle: *Fort Street engineers fitting a new generator to the **Peveril** [4] which necessitated cutting a hole in the vehicle deck and severing numerous ducts and diverting pipework to get the equipment into place in the engine room. (Charlie Coole)*

Bottom: *The staff pose in front of a vehicle ramp which they manufactured for use at Belfast, showing the diversity of work undertaken under their workshop manager Charlie Coole who sits appropriately at the top of the pile! (I.O.M.S.P.Co.)*

Top: *Two interesting views of the water-jet propulsion units of the* **SeaCat Isle of Man** *removed during dry-docking. The vessel has four such units mounted in pairs on each hull. The picture on the top right shows where they are located in the hull. (I.O.M.S.P.Co.)*

Middle: *One of the four main Ruston 16-cylinder engines in the engine space on the* **SeaCat Isle of Man,** *illustrating the cramped conditions making it virtually impossible to work on them whilst at sea. All engine controls are monitored by the Duty Engineer remotely on the bridge of the vessel. (I.O.M.S.P.Co.)*

Bottom: *When the* **Peveril** *[4] first arrived on charter as* **NF Jaguar** *the vessel had no belting. After purchase in 1993 steel belting was fitted to the vessel to protect the hull shell plating from damage when entering Hornby Dock in the Liverpool dock system. In this photograph Fort Street engineers are repairing damage to the belting at Douglas. (I.O.M.S.P.Co.)*

*The **Seacat Isle of Man** in dry dock for her annual survey. (Dick Clague)*

*The **SuperSeaCat Three** in dry dock for annual survey showing her monohull construction and the four water-jet propulsion units placed in line across the hull. Note the absence of conventional rudders, steering being effected by steerable jets and astern direction using clam buckets not unlike the reverse thrust on a jet aircraft. A stark contrast to all that has gone before. (Dick Clague)*

*The **Lady of Mann** (2) in Bidston dry dock for annual survey and undergoing repair to her bow rudder so much a feature of the Steam Packet ships before the introduction of bow thrusters when their vessels had to use astern navigation leaving Douglas and on approach to other ports. (Dick Clague)*

LADY OF MANN

*The photograph taken on 26th January 1985 (above) shows **Mona's Isle** (6) in dry dock at Govan in company with her former consort **Free Enterprise IV** which has just completed a re-fit. The **Mona's Isle** (6) was there to undergo major alterations to equip her for service with the Steam Packet including the fitting of additional lounge accommodation on the boat deck aft with progress seen as at 10th March 1985 (below) just under a month before she entered service. (Lawrence Macduff)*

*A wonderful photograph of **Ben-my-Chree** [4] in Brocklebank Graving Dock. It shows the lines of the counter stern and the fine underwater lines of the traditional ships to good effect. Alas neither the ship nor the dock is any more, the former scrapped and the latter filled in. (Ian Collard)*

The **Tynwald** [5] in Bidston Graving Dock for annual survey which was a requirement for passenger ship certification. The photograph shows the bow rudder hard over to allow inspection of the bearings. (Ian Collard)

*This photograph of **Ben-my-Chree** (4) drifting in past the Battery Pier with astern steam just being bled on by the engineers in anticipation of the forthcoming manoeuvre as she comes alongside the Victoria Pier. The photograph was taken in 1965, her last year of operation, and captures the essence of a lost era. (Jim Lace)*

*It is hard to believe that **Snaefell** (5) is still on summer service as she makes a lumpy approach to Douglas harbour in a south-easterly gale in August 1973. (Stan Basnett)*

*The **Snaefell** (5) has a difficult approach in August 1968 to Number 1 berth on the Victoria Pier ahead of the **Lady of Mann** (1) as an easterly breeze will push her off the pier as she loses way. There was no bow thruster then to push the head in! (Stan Basnett)*

*The **Lady of Mann** (1) takes a 09.00 sailing to Liverpool at the end of September 1965 with returning competitors and spectators after the International Six Day Motorcycle Trial which was held on the Island that year. (Stan Basnett)*

*A superb photograph of the **Mona** (4) and the twin funnel **Ramsey Town** in winter, laid up at the Tongue in Douglas inner harbour sometime in the early 1930s. The Douglas Head steam ferry **Thistle** is also seen in the photograph. (Richard Davis collection)*

*The **Tynwald** [4] - a classic shot of one of the pre-war sister ships which were to pave the way for the post-war passenger vessels. The basic hull form is established as is the layout which was not destined to change substantially until the advent of the first car ferries in 1962. (Bruce Peter collection)*

CHAPTER FOUR

Called up for Service

So much has been written about the involvement of the Steam Packet personnel and vessels in the two major conflicts that it is difficult to avoid repetition. Following the outbreak of hostilities in 1914 the Steam Packet Co. was requested to send full details of the fleet to the Admiralty. Comprehensive details of the fifteen vessels owned by the Company were sent by C. J. Blackburn the Superintendent Engineer on 24th December 1914. Eleven were either purchased or chartered for use by the Admiralty. At the end of hostilities only four returned to the Company to continue their normal trade. *Peel Castle*, *King Orry* (3), *Mona's Queen* (3) and *Viking*.

The *Peel Castle* was commissioned as an armed boarding vessel under the White Ensign in November 1914 and manned by R.N.V.R personnel and all the engineering staff from the Steam Packet. All alterations and fitting out was done at Cammell Laird & Co. at Birkenhead.

She left the Mersey on 22nd November under sealed orders for Scapa Flow to undertake gunnery trials before heading for Plymouth to become part of the Dover Patrol under Admiral Bacon. A normal patrol was ten days at sea and four days in port at Dover. While on patrol her normal duty was stop and search but as submarine activity increased, the rescue of crews from torpedoed ships became an equally important function.

Disaster struck on 7th February 1916 when fire broke out on the *Peel Castle* in the middle of the night in a store above the magazine. Fire parties tackled the fire and flooded the magazine but they were unable to contain the fire. The salvage tug *Lady Brassey* responded and eventually the fire was subdued but not before completely gutting all of the central accommodation. The crew had abandoned the vessel and it was discovered that one member was missing.

The next day the captain and some crew returned to the vessel and doused remaining fires in the bunkers and at other locations. They also discovered the body of the interpreter in the gutted accommodation. A week later the Peel Castle was towed to Chatham Dockyard for refit and returned to her duties in the Downs six weeks later.

Early in 1918 she was sent to Leith where she received further alterations. The boat deck was extended to form a landing deck for a Kite Balloon and associated winch gear. Depth charge throwers and paravanes were fitted at the same time. On completion of the work the *Peel Castle* was deployed on convoy work on the Norweigan convoys and

*The **Manxman** was not purchased by the Company from the Midland Railway until 1920 but it too was called up for service like the **Viking** and **Ben-my-Chree** [3] and all were converted to seaplane carriers. After the loss of the **Ben-my-Chree** [3] in January 1917 the **Manxman** and the **Viking** served together in the Eastern Mediterranean for the last year of the war and were de-commissioned together in 1919. (Imperial War Museum)*

*The **Snaefell** [3] as a First World War armed boarding vessel, a duty to which several coastal steamers were allocated. Towards the end of the War she was engaged in trooping in the Mediterranean. She did not return, being sunk by torpedo in 1918. (Imperial War Museum)*

*In World War 2 the **Viking** was also converted at Liverpool to perform the same duty as the **Ben-my-Chree** [3] and in the same theatre of war but survived. Having been bought by the Admiralty for the duration she was renamed HMS **Vindex**. The Company bought the vessel back on completion of hostilities. The ship did serve the country a second time. (Imperial War Museum)*

called up for service

The **Ben-my-Chree** [4] *in wartime camouflage as a Landing Ship (Infantry) with the mainmast removed to allow the sweep of an anti-aircraft gun with which she was fitted. (Stan Basnett collection)*

later on the Humber – Tyne convoys.

At the cessation of hostilities she returned to Liverpool in January 1919 and was fitted out for troop carrying at Cammell Laird's. She was then sent to the Channel. Finally she returned to Birkenhead, had all fittings put back for peacetime work and returned to the Steam Packet.

The *King Orry* (3) was also fitted out as an armed boarding vessel at Birkenhead in November 1914 and stationed at Scapa Flow patrolling the Pentland Firth, the Skaggerak, the Orkneys and the area off Peterhead and Kirkwall. It was quickly discovered that the belting on her was a problem when lowering and retrieving the boarding boats so she returned to Birkenhead to have it removed.

Her work took her to dangerous waters off the German minefields near Heligoland and in the Skaggerak where she continued her stop and search role. Following the loss of the *Ramsey* whilst employed on similar duties the *King Orry* (3) had her 12 pounder removed and was fitted with two 4" guns mounted on the port and starboard quarter and an anti-aircraft gun added.

After her patrol work at the Battle of Jutland the vessel sustained bottom damage on 9th June 1915 whilst negotiating the Sound of Islay. Fortunately the tank top remained intact but the starboard propeller and steering gear were damaged. Temporary steering gear was rigged and the ship proceeded under one engine to Birkenhead for

repair. She was fitted with towing gear, returned to Scapa Flow, and deployed towing the largest targets for gunnery practice with the battleships firing from a range of ten miles. As each was out of sight of the other it is not surprising that it was an extremely hazardous occupation and the *King Orry* was hit on one occasion by a 6" shell which passed through the hull above the waterline fortunately without any casualties.

Late in 1916 she was to change her role yet again effectively becoming a Q ship disguised as a cargo vessel by the addition of derricks and a temporary superstructure and with her name changed to *Viking Orry*. A further visit to Birkenhead was necessary to repair damage and have her bow strengthened caused by heavy weather encountered off the Northern Isles. After repair she returned to Scapa Flow and the same duties.

The *King Orry* (3) achieved a degree of fame in November 1918 as the only representative of the British mercantile fleet present at the surrender of the German Fleet at Scapa Flow where she occupied a place in the convoy as a repeater ship. The ship was commanded by Navy Personnel throughout.

The *Mona's Queen* (2) was chartered by the Admiralty in March 1915 and prepared for trooping at Douglas by the Company's employees. She was engaged solely on trooping mainly between Southampton and Le Havre. Capt Cain

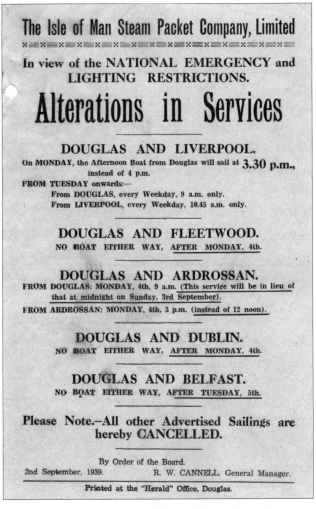

The Isle of Man Steam Packet Company, Limited

×=×=×=×=×=×=×=×=×=×=×=×=×=×=×=×=×=×

In view of the NATIONAL EMERGENCY and
LIGHTING RESTRICTIONS.

Alterations in Services

DOUGLAS AND LIVERPOOL.
On MONDAY, the Afternoon Boat from Douglas will sail at **3.30 p.m.,**
instead of 4 p.m.
FROM TUESDAY onwards:—
From DOUGLAS, every Weekday, 9 a.m. only.
From LIVERPOOL, every Weekday, 10.45 a.m. only.

DOUGLAS AND FLEETWOOD.
NO BOAT EITHER WAY, AFTER MONDAY, 4th.

DOUGLAS AND ARDROSSAN.
FROM DOUGLAS: MONDAY, 4th, 9 a.m. (This service will be in lieu of
that at midnight on Sunday, 3rd September).
FROM ARDROSSAN: MONDAY, 4th, 3 p.m. (instead of 12 noon).

DOUGLAS AND DUBLIN.
NO BOAT EITHER WAY, AFTER MONDAY, 4th.

DOUGLAS AND BELFAST.
NO BOAT EITHER WAY, AFTER TUESDAY, 5th.

**Please Note.—All other Advertised Sailings are
hereby CANCELLED.**

By Order of the Board.
2nd September, 1939.   R. W. CANNELL, General Manager.

Printed at the "Herald" Office, Douglas.

*A public notice from the Company which was the first indication that services
would be severely affected by the outbreak of war. (Manx National Heritage)*

for peacetime service and returned to the company in 1920 becoming the last paddler in of the fleet.

The *Viking* was requisitioned by the Admiralty in March 1915 and purchased by them later that year. She was extensively converted at Birkenhead by Cammell Laird & Co. almost beyond recognition to become a seaplane carrier, to carry four seaplanes and four single seat fighters.

The work involved removing the boat deck aft of the funnels and building a large hangar and workshop, fitting two large cranes for retrieving the aircraft from the sea after returning from missions (even the fighters which had conventional landing gear had to land on the water and deploy floatation bags and await recovery).

The mainmast was removed and replaced with two masts on each side of the take off runway and fitted with lifting gear. On commissioning, her name was changed to *HMS Vindex* as the Navy already had an F class destroyer *HMS Viking*. The vessel served in the North Sea before operating in the eastern Mediterranean in 1918. De-commissioned in March 1919 the Steam Packet Co. bought her back and after being restored to her original condition she resumed her normal duties on the Fleetwood service.

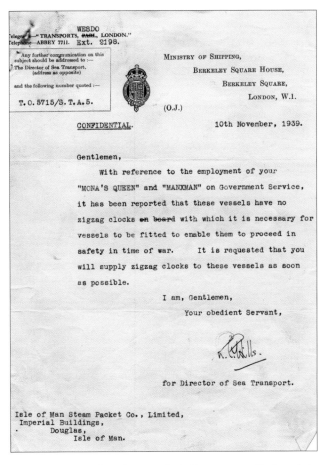

*It is quite amazing to learn that it was for the Company to provide zigzag clocks
to enable the ships to perform zigzag manoeuvres when in convoy formation, at
their own cost in their vessels which had been requisitioned by the Admiralty.
(Manx National Heritage)*

remained in command and George Kenna was retained as Chief Engineer.

On 6th February 1917 on passage to Le Havre with more than a thousand men on board she came under attack from a surfaced U-boat which fired a torpedo that passed underneath her thanks to her shallow draft. The *Mona's Queen* continued at full speed and struck the submarine with her port paddle wheel damaging the paddles and unseating the main drive shaft bearing. At first it was thought that the submarine had sunk but although damaged ahead of the conning tower it survived and returned to service after repair.

The *Mona's Queen* (2) continued at reduced speed and discharged her troops at Le Havre, returning to Southampton under her own power escorted by two destroyers and a tug. It was found that despite the impact the 19" diameter paddle wheel shaft was not bent. Repairs to the paddle wheel and the hull plating were carried out by Harland and Wolff at Southampton and she returned to service in the Channel in March.

The *Mona's Queen* was de-commissioned in April 1919 and left Southampton for Birkenhead to be reconditioned

The **Fenella** [2] *and the* **Tynwald** [4] *were engaged in trooping in the early months of 1940 between Southampton and the French ports of Le Havre and Cherbourg.* (*Imperial War Museum*)

The **Lady of Mann** [1] *was employed in Operations Cycle and Aerial and is photographed at Brest in June 1940 loaded beyond capacity and awaiting departure.* (*Imperial War Museum*)

The *Ben-my-Chree* (3) was requisitioned and chartered by the Government on 1st January 1915 and underwent coversion to a seaplane carrier at Birkenhead like the *Viking*. A large hangar was constructed on the after boat deck and two masts with heavy derricks fitted to lift the sea planes back on board. A large maintenance workshop was constructed on the shelter deck below.

After commissioning she left for her base at Harwich from where she was deployed off the Belgian Coast spotting for submarine activity. In May 1915 she left for the Dardanelles and was engaged in target location for the British battleships followed by various deployments off Egypt, Turkey and Bulgaria.

By February 1917 she was back off the island of Castellorizo at anchor in what was supposed to be a safe haven when she was hit by a salvo of shells from the mainland some two miles away. Fire could not be returned because of the high elevation of the battery. The damage and resulting fire led to the *Ben-my-Chree* becoming a total loss. Fortunately all the crew and servicemen abandoned ship and were saved. Shelling continued until she sank.

The paddle steamer *Mona's Isle* (3) was purchased by the Admiralty in September 1915 and was sent to Barrow to be fitted out as a net-laying and anti-submarine ship by Vickers.

Back in the Isle of Man Cunningham's Holiday Camp was requisitioned as an internment camp and eventually housed 2,600 enemy aliens. Another camp was purpose built near Peel and that eventually housed 26,000 internees and 2,500 guards. On 17th November 1914 the *Tynwald* (4) brought in the first of what was to become (part of her regular duty).

During the full period of the conflict the *Tynwald* maintained the service between Liverpool and the Island carrying the mails, military personnel and whatever passengers that were travelling. During that time she maintained the vital link without incident, despite the constant risk of mines in the Mersey and its approaches. She was also called upon to carry extra troops to Ireland as required calling for some fairly intense working.

In 1938 the same request came from the Ministry of War Transport for details of the Steam Packet fleet. Once again the Superintendent Engineer, now Mr R. B. Moore, supplied full details of the sixteen vessels owned by the Company; eleven were requisitioned initially, eight for use as troop transporters (with the *Victoria* following later) and three to become armed boarding vessels.

The outbreak of hostilities coincided with the end of the 1939 tourist season which had been overshadowed by the impending threat of war. By August some of the Steam Packet vessels had already been requisitioned, others were following for the usual lay-up with doubts as to what was going to happen. There was to be no respite in the coming winter of 1939/40: the call came sooner than expected.

The *Viking* had been docked at Barrow since the end of August and left for Southampton on 7th September 1939, war having been declared on the 3rd. Two days later *Lady of Mann* [1], *Ben-my-Chree* [4] and *Snaefell* [4] all left Barrow for Liverpool and then Southampton for trooping duties to Cherbourg. This time the vessels would operate as troop transports with their own civilian crews and military liaison officers on board to control troop movements. The intensity of the workload under extremely dangerous conditions would eventually take its toll on the crews who had received no training in defence and had just been thrown in at the deep end. The ships that were initially classed as troop transports were sent to Dover to become part of the Ministry of War Transport's South East Coast Ports Pool and were immediately put to work conveying the British Army to France.

Bertram Ramsay was on the Retired List at the outbreak of war but was called up and appointed Vice Admiral Dover, answerable directly to the Board of Admiralty. His initial task was to organise the movement of troops and supplies across the Channel but following the invasion of France in May 1940 he realised that he was not going to supply an army but rescue it, for which task he had just seven days' notice. Code-named Operation Dynamo the evacuation of the British Army was to centre on Dover, Folkestone, Calais and Dunkirk. The Steam Packet vessels were to be in the thick of it. Initially it was thought that it would involve the evacuation of 45,000 troops but in the end the figure reached an astonishing 338,000!

Most of the transports were converted after the evacuation to Landing Ships (Infantry)(LSI), being fitted with hand-hoisted landing craft. Their missions took some as far north as Iceland and the Faeroes and as far south as the Mediterranean.

It must be remembered that all of the crews of these vessels were Merchant Navy officers and seamen, not military personnel but included some Channel pilots. They were suddenly flung into a major theatre of war with no effective defence against air attack and bombardment from shore batteries other than some cover provided by the escort destroyers also engaged in the evacuation operation. There was no air cover against the constant attack from the Luftwaffe and no protection of the East Pier at Dunkirk from which the larger draught cross-channel vessels could only operate.

More than sixty-five years on from that time it is almost impossible to imagine the trauma experienced by men of the Company and those of other cross-channel companies involved in Operation Dynamo which lasted for ten days from 26th May to 4th June 1940. There was intense activity over a four-day period with crews getting little or no rest. Understandably tensions ran high and there was inevitable conflict with the Admiralty Sea Transport Officers at Folkestone, many of whom were reservists without seagoing experience and to whom the ships were just names and numbers placed on the sailing schedules.

Captain W. Qualtrough of the *Tynwald* [4] was one of several Masters of the personnel and transport ships who informed the Admiralty STO at Folkestone that he and his deck officers had had little more than four hours' sleep in

*The **Manx Maid** [1] was also at Brest for the evacuations from Brittany and berthed next to the **Lady of Mann** (1). Both ships were loaded to capacity and were delayed due to air raids and minelaying activity in the harbour and the approach channel. (Imperial War Museum)*

the whole week. Their request for relief was refused. Despite this they continued to participate in the evacuation; inevitably there were those who broke down and just could not continue. Imagine though the plight of the engine room staff who had no idea of what conditions were like above deck. How those men endured this time is beyond comprehension, knowing as they did the fate of many of their colleagues in the loss of the *Mona's Queen* [3] which had been mined on 29th May. In the same period the Admiralty withdrew eight of their larger H, I and J class destroyers due to their 'vulnerability'! Meanwhile the unarmed transports remained exposed to constant attack. The destroyers also had the luxury of crew changes during the period which further exacerbated the situation.

The Steam Packet vessels involved in the May/June 1940 evacuation from France and the Channel Islands are credited with the following figures:

Viking rescued 6,600 troops from Cherbourg, Le Havre and Guernsey and completed four return trips. A fifth trip was made light-ship from Le Havre to Cherbourg.

King Orry [3] rescued 1,139 troops from Dunkirk and was sunk on the second trip.

Manxman [1] rescued 5,754 troops and completed six return trips to Dunkirk, St. Malo and Cherbourg.

Mona's Isle [4] rescued 2,630 troops from Dunkirk and completed two return trips.

Manx Maid [1] rescued 2,090 troops from Brest to Plymouth and completed one return trip.

Ben-my-Chree [4] rescued 3,845 troops and completed three return trips to Dunkirk.

Lady of Mann [1] rescued 7,207 troops and completed seven return trips to Dunkirk, Cherbourg, Brest and La Pallice.

Mona's Queen [3] rescued 3,398 troops and completed three return trips to Ostend, Boulogne and Dunkirk but was sunk on her second trip to Dunkirk.

Tynwald [4] rescued 9,680 troops and completed five return trips to Dunkirk and two to Cherbourg.

The *Fenella* [2] was sunk at Dunkirk without rescuing any troops.

Many of the human stories, however, are often forgotten. Through reference to local newspapers, unpublished manuscripts and anecdotal accounts we hope to present a slightly different view of the work undertaken by the Steam Packet vessels and crews. Some of their exploits do not even appear in the official records held in the National Archive for what often seem like bizarre reasons. However, as with all historical accounts the real story always lies beneath the surface and with the people that have made the Company what it is. Their story is sometimes tragic, often serious, occasionally sad and fortunately for everyone sometimes humorous.

Take for example one of the missions undertaken by *Manxman* [1] as recalled by the late Captain Tom Corteen who was Second Mate on the vessel at the time of the Dunkirk evacuation -

"I was both Mate and Second Mate of the *Manxman* that week as the original Mate had a nervous breakdown on our first run over. There was quite a lot of action around Dunkirk at the time so then I had everything to see to and organise which was a full-time job.

The *Manxman* (1) did four runs to Dunkirk, one of which we may not have been credited with as on arrival off Dunkirk at daylight – Thursday I think – the operation was cancelled owing to the very heavy shelling taking place. The five other channel vessels with us were turned back by a destroyer, the *Lady of Mann* (1) was one of them, but as we had been in the lead we were never contacted owing to the thick easterly haze and heavy smoke drifting down over the Channel from the burning town and the burning fuel tanks.

So we entered the harbour not knowing that we were on our own. It was very eerie steaming in. There was not a soldier to be seen either on the beaches or on the Mole. They had all been pulled back into the town as there was no shelter from the bursting shells out in the open. There was no Naval officer on the Mole to berth us, no personnel to take our ropes but underneath the Mole was packed solid with soldiers perched and straddled on the piles some up to their chins in water - all out of sight to miss as much of the shrapnel and strafing as possible although the Mole was hit several times.

Some soldiers had been washed off the piles as the tide made – there was no room on the piles above them. They didn't understand tides and how the tide swept through the piled Mole. Incidentally we had quite a job to get berthed alongside, getting soldiers to take two or three turns of a light six-inch rope around a pile and then hang onto the eye whilst we could heave her alongside when a sailor could jump onto the piles and make our rope secure. We cut these ropes with a fire axe on leaving.

We embarked every soldier – a very long job as they all had to worm their way along the piles even from the inner end of the Mole, using some of our gangways to bridge the gaps made by the shellfire and shells were screaming overhead all the time.

When we arrived back at Dover a destroyer came racing out to meet us as we had been given up, having been missing all day. There was no one down in Dover to see us berth, seeing that the evacuation had been cancelled that day. No Army or Navy personnel, no reporters, no trains laid on so the soldiers just lay down on the quayside and slept awaiting transport.

How anyone arrived at numbers carried

amazes me as the soldiers came on at the Mole any way they could and not all by gangways or planks and no one was counting anyway. On arrival at Dover or Folkestone they just swarmed ashore, the destroyers or other vessels unloading their troops over us at the same time. It was just one continuous flood of men pouring ashore.

Again some vessels would be in and out of Dunkirk in two or three hours if the troops were down in great numbers so it was the actual time spent in the place that mattered, not the number of times in and out. The tension would ease every time one was leaving the place because it was in and around Dunkirk that the heavy action was taking place.

Another day we were on the point of leaving Dunkirk with a full load of troops when some of the crew who were standing by ready to let go came running up to me in a very distressed state. A destroyer had tied up alongside us and moored up to our lifeboat deflectors and our troops were naturally swarming down on board of her. She took nearly all of them, in fact she had to cast off or she would have been overwhelmed. I told the destroyer commander what I thought about the whole business - him robbing us of our troops when we were on the point of leaving and the way he had upset the crew after the harrowing time that they had just been through.

The destroyer left after only minutes alongside while we had to wait at the Mole again while more troops were rounded up and sent down to us as no troops were left on the Mole unless there was a vessel there to receive them. This destroyer left us as the only vessel in – nothing even outside the pier heads. So we were alone with no protection, not even a pop gun and not a single tin hat amongst us. In fact no soldier would lend me his tin hat when I had to go forward to pin the bow rudder and I asked quite a few.

Whilst we were lying alongside, Hugh Crennell, the lamp-trimmer who had been a gunner in the 1914-18 war, procured a Lewis gun and a box of ammunition from some of the troops. I helped him set it up foreside of the bridge and also helped to load many pans of ammunition with practically all tracer bullets. He used that gun quite a few times before we got away and he was turning the screaming Stukas off course. I could see bullets passing straight through them and their bombs were falling clear of us. I did not realise it at the time that they would be machine-gunning us! Without that gun I am sure that we would never have got out of Dunkirk and I mentioned this to Admiral Ramsay back in Dover but 'lamps' had cracked up on the passage and had to go ashore.

During the early part of the week quite a

few soldiers had died on passage as there was no medical attention. Some on board were killed or wounded by their own mates who on getting on board us were clearing their rifles from the top deck by placing the muzzle down on the wooden deck and pulling the trigger. I was hoarse going round the top deck shouting for them to clear their rifles over the side or in the air. I had not slept for a week, my nerves had kept me going and Admiral Ramsay relieved me with a Naval officer but the evacuation ended that day.

I saw the *Mona's Queen* mined and break in two from her stern to her mainmast. We were very close to her – in fact we had passed over the same spot shortly before and we were then just stemming the tide awaiting a berth at the Mole. Her degaussing may have failed - she had the electric wires around her hull whilst we were wiped: she did not strike a mine.

We also stopped several times on our passage to pick up soldiers who were trying to row ships' lifeboats across the Channel and these took time, most of them right in the Dunkirk area. The last time we left Dunkirk we steamed straight out across the sandbanks seeing that the tide would probably give us enough water, as the east and west buoyed channels were strewn with wrecks and we also presented a much smaller target for the shellfire which was still taking place.

On another trip leaving Dunkirk the bosun came to tell me that a destroyer berthed astern of us on leaving whilst swinging on a wire rope on the ebbing tide had been set a long way up the Mole and the Navy personnel on the Mole had not been able to lift the eye of the wire rope over the pile which was about five feet high to let go. The destroyer just threw his end of the wire rope over the side thus shutting us in as the wire lay in a parabola from the top of the Mole which was about thirty feet above sea level to well across the harbour. I had to call for at least six volunteers to go ashore with me along the Mole to pull enough slack back on this wire to lift the eye over the pile and dump it into the harbour - a hard pull along the muddy bottom. Without clearing this wire we would have picked it up with our propellers on leaving stern first. Fortunately the bosun Vernon Stewart had been watching the destroyer casting off and swinging."

A similar experience concerning the exposed position of ships at Dunkirk is described by T.K. Cannell who was a young officer on the *Ben-my-Chree* [4]. While berthed at the East Mole at Dunkirk on 31st May he recalled -

"The ship's gangways were out, I expected men would soon be pouring aboard but it was not working. Groups of soldiers would come running down the Mole, sometimes groups would walk, sometimes injured would be carried aboard and the stretchers laid on deck and sometimes there would be no troops at all coming aboard. Later they confirmed their reluctance to approach the ship due to the intensity of the attacks on her. The explosions of the bombs sounded very close."

The ship was a sitting duck, totally defenceless, and clearly everyone was frightened - it was pure luck that she did not receive a direct hit.

The *Viking* which had seen active service in the First World War when she was converted almost beyond recognition as a seaplane carrier also found herself commandeered for service in the Second. One of her lesser-known exploits, relying purely on anecdotal account, would have gone unnoticed prior to 2002 if it had not been for Mrs Audrey Mansell, the daughter of the ship's Master Captain 'Ginger' Bridson.

The story concerns the evacuation of children from the island of Guernsey in 1940. As always happens we are often told things by our parents when we are young which leave a lasting impression, but it is not until we are older ourselves that we realise what we have been told and we want to find out more and often it is too late. This was the case with the Captain's daughter.

It is easier for me to let her set the scene herself by quoting firstly from a speech she gave before the Bailiff of Guernsey and the Viking Evacuees Group at a presentation in Guernsey and then in full the account recalled by Captain Kinley -

"My Father was in the Royal Navy during the First World War. He served in HMS *Malaya* at the Battle of Jutland and then on minesweepers. He left the Navy after the war and joined the Isle of Man Steam Packet Company in the early '20s.

At the outbreak of war in September 1939 he was Master of the *Viking* which was commissioned by the Royal Navy to serve as a troopship ferrying our troops from Southampton to the French Ports. But in the early months of 1940 the tide of war turned as the Germans invaded France and the *Viking* began a reverse role of evacuating British troops from Cherbourg, Le Havre, St. Valery and St. Malo to Southampton and Portsmouth. They made many trips under fire from German planes each time but they were successful, carrying over 2,000 troops every time.

It was during this hazardous operation - on June 20th - that he was ordered to sail to Guernsey in the Channel Islands and to evacuate the schoolchildren and their teachers to Weymouth. He told me this story many times and as a small child myself at the time I found it very moving. He described it as the most momentous event of his

NOTICE.

I am instructed to inform the people of Guernsey that the Government of the United Kingdom has decided that this Bailiwick is to be entirely demilitarised.

Accordingly, the Royal Court hereby gives instructions for the immediate demobilisation of the Royal Guernsey Militia and of the Guernsey Defence Volunteers.

Arms, uniforms and equipment are forthwith to be handed in at the Town Arsenal under arrangements to be made by the Officers Commanding the Royal Guernsey Militia and the Guernsey Defence Volunteers, to be disposed of in accordance with the instructions of the Officer Commanding Troops Guernsey and Alderney District.

All ranks of the Militia and all members of the Guernsey Defence Volunteers will then proceed quietly to their homes.

All other persons in possession of firearms must forthwith hand them to the Constable of their Parish who will take immediate steps to have them transported to the Town Arsenal.

VICTOR G. CAREY,
Bailiff of Guernsey

entire life at sea. He was so afraid, he said, in case they didn't make it. Soldiers are one thing, he said, but children - innocent children - were something else.

If I may I would like to read an account of the event which was written by the late Captain Harry Kinley who as a young man was Second Officer on board the *Viking* at the time".

The Evacuation of the Children of Guernsey - June 21st 1940, written by Captain Harry Kinley

"My name is Harry Kinley and in 1940, aged 30, I was Second Officer on board the *Viking*, an Isle of Man Steam Packet Company passenger ship which had been commissioned by the Navy as a troopship. We were evacuating troops from the French Channel ports to Southampton, when we were ordered to proceed to Guernsey and to evacuate as many of the schoolchildren and their teachers as possible. Navigating the waters around the Channel Islands was difficult but fortunately I had kept all the charts up to date and we had a

THE RATIONS

Rations for the journey: Sandwiches (egg or cheese); Packets of nuts and seedless raisins; Dry biscuits (with little packets of cheese); Barley sugar (rather than chocolate); Apple; Orange.

Parents of children to be evacuated must attend at the school attended by their children at 9 a.m. to-morrow, the 20th June, to receive instructions as to the final arrangements to be complied with.

Parents of children under school age will attend at the Parish School of the Parish in which they reside at 10 a.m. to-morrow, the 20th June, to receive similar instructions.

Persons willing to accompany evacuated children as helpers should give their names and addresses to any headmaster or headmistress.

It will not be possible, on account of the danger of air raids, to permit masses of people to congregate at the harbour and accordingly parents must say au-revoir to their children at their homes or at the Schools. The public will not be permitted to approach the harbour.

Transport to the harbour will be provided as necessary.

On registration for the evacuation of children or adults, it must be stated whether or not financial provision can be made for the maintenance of the evacuee in the United Kingdom and whether or not the evacuee can go to a relative or friend there and the name and address of that relative or friend must be given.

VICTOR G. CAREY,
Bailiff of Guernsey.

very good ship's Master, Captain James Bridson. We docked without trouble at No. 1 Berth in St. Peter Port at 4 a.m. on June 21st.

By 9 a.m., the children were arriving in great numbers and I will never forget the sight of those thousands of children lined up on the pier with their gas masks over their shoulders and carrying small cases. From the age of four to seventeen they came aboard, many of them in tears. It was hard to keep back our own tears, I can tell you. We stopped counting the children after 1,800 and with the teachers and helpers there must have been well over 2,000 on board.

The ship was packed; every cabin, corner and space was filled. Going around talking to the children, I found that they had been waiting so long that most of them had eaten the food their parents had packed for them. They were hungry poor mites. I went to Captain Bridson to report and he told me to strip the lifeboats of the provisions and distribute them among the children. Together with the crew, I went round with sweets, cake, biscuits and even condensed milk which we dished out in spoonfuls!

In my own cabin there were at least a dozen little ones with their Sunday School teacher. This lady gave me her prayer book and I gave her my Merchant Navy badge. Another lady gave her front door key to Ned Gelling, our Chief Officer, and asked him to lock her front door if the ship went back to Guernsey, because she had forgotten to do so!

We finally set sail at 11 a.m. Because we were a coal-burning ship we were very conspicuous and a passing warship signalled a message: "You are a pillar of smoke by day and a ball of fire by night and can be seen for twenty miles." We signalled back: "Thank you, we know." There were mines in the Channel and enemy aircraft overhead and we had one old gun and no escort. A plane did swoop down over us, which caused a bit of panic, but it was one of ours which made the children cheer. We said our prayers and zigzagged across to England with our precious cargo, eventually landing safely at Weymouth, where crowds on the quayside sent up a cheer. As the children disembarked, I was standing with Captain Bridson at the gangway saying goodbye and I said to him, "I wonder what will become of them all?" "So do I, Harry", he said, "I wish we could sail on to the Isle of Man with them, they would be safe there."

From Weymouth, the children were put onto trains and taken, with their school teachers, to many parts of England and Scotland, where they were to remain for the next five years, as it transpired. But for many of the children the separation from Guernsey was to be much longer. They never went back and the island lost a significant part of a generation. Curiously enough, some years later, my niece married a young man from Glasgow, who turned out to be one of those very same Guernsey children who had been evacuated on the *Viking*. He had not returned to Guernsey after the war but had come to live in the Isle of Man with the family he had been billeted with.

A Manxman, born and raised on a small island - and a father - I could well imagine the feelings of those parents. Fearful of the German invasion and not knowing what lay ahead, they made that heart-breaking decision to send the children away for their own safety. I had many memorable experiences during the war years and a lifetime at sea, but one I shall never forget is the evacuation of the children of Guernsey".

Thanks be to God we made it.

The *Guernsey Evening Press* dated Wednesday 19th June 1940 had carried a notice notifying parents of young children of arrangements for their evacuation. The notice directed parents of schoolchildren to attend at their school at 7 p.m. to notify their willingness or otherwise for the evacuation of their children. Parents of under-school-age children who wanted them to be evacuated were required to register with the Rector or Vicar of their Parish by 8 p.m. The lists so prepared were to be delivered to the Bailiff's Office by 10 p.m.

Arrangements were also made for other classes who wished to be evacuated and parents of the under-age children who wished to accompany them. The notice stated that evacuation was to take place on Thursday 20th.

Many parents got less than three hours' notice in which to make their decision which must have been traumatic and heart-breaking.

A list of basic clothing as laid down in the notice amounted to one change of clothing and a coat! The notice also stipulated the rations for the journey: sandwiches (egg or cheese); packets of nuts and seedless raisins; dry biscuits (with little packets of cheese); barley sugar (rather than chocolate); apple; orange. Parents had to attend school the following morning at 9 a.m. for their final instructions.

Parents were told that they would have to say goodbye to their children either at home or at school as they would not be allowed to approach the harbour.

We cannot imagine what this must have been like for the children other than to read the recollection that Captain Kinley had as Second Mate of the *Viking* when she arrived at St. Peter Port in the early hours of 21st June to take these people to Weymouth and then for them to go to destinations all over Britain. Some recollections of evacuees follow.

Recollections of Evacuation from Guernsey

- June 1940

The first recollection is from Arthur Laine, who was mentioned by Captain Kinley -

"My earliest recollection is of being on a beach with my mother one afternoon, when a lady came along and told us to return home immediately, pack a small suitcase and report to my school, St. Samson's Boys - I was seven years old.

On arrival at the school we were told that we were going to England on a boat. This caused great excitement as we had never been off the island. Being seven years old the implications of this event did not register.

From school we marched in "crocodile" to White Rock and awaited the arrival of the boat. We waited for ages and finally boarded a boat, the name of which I did not find out until many years later. I remember that I was with a group in a small cabin with a teacher and we had been sailing for a while when the sailors came around and to our great delight handed out sweets, chocolates and biscuits, which we thought had come from a shop.

PARENTS MUST REPORT THIS EVENING

Clothing and Ration Necessities

Arrangements are being made for the evacuation of (1) children of school age and (2) children under school age to reception areas in the United Kingdom under Government arrangement.

The evacuation is expected to take place to-morrow, the 20th June, 1940.

The mothers of children under school age will be allowed to accompany their children.

Parents of schoolchildren are to attend at the school attended by their children at 7 p.m. to-day to notify their willingness or otherwise for the evacuation of their children.

IF PARENTS DESIRE IT

Parents of children under school age who desire their children evacuated must give the name and address of such children to the Rector or Vicar of their Parish by 8 p.m. to-day. The Rectors will prepare lists accordingly and will transmit them by 10 p.m. to the Bailiff's Office.

Other persons (other than men of military age) desirous of being evacuated must register their names and addresses with the Constables of their Parish at the Parish Douzaine Room as soon as possible and at latest by 8 p.m. to-day.

All men of military age, i.e., from 20 to 33 years, who desire to be evacuated must register their names and addresses with the Constables of their Parish at the Parish Douzaine Room by 9 p.m. THEY ARE VERY STRONGLY URGED TO DO SO.

ARTICLES TO TAKE

Children should take with them on evacuation the following articles:—

Gas masks.
Two ration books (current and new one).

Besides the clothes which the child will be wearing, which should include an overcoat or mackintosh, a complete change of clothing should be carried. The following is suggested:—

GIRLS	BOYS
One vest or combination.	One vest.
One pair of knickers.	One shirt with collar.
One bodice.	One pair of pants.
One petticoat.	One pullover or jersey.
Two pairs of stockings.	One pair of knickers.
Handkerchiefs.	Handkerchifs.
Slip and blouse.	Two pairs of socks or stockings.
Cardigan.	

Night attire, comb, towel, soap, face-cloth, tooth-

This event was of great significance to me as I will explain later.

After many hours at sea we finally landed at the port of Weymouth. From here we were put on trains, and after what seemed like days I, along with others from my school, arrived in Glasgow and were taken to a church hall in a place called Cardonald which is between Paisley and Glasgow. We slept on camp beds and on the very first night there was an air raid in which Crawfords biscuit factory in Paisley was set on fire. I remember the whole sky was lit up - it was very frightening. That was our introduction to life as an evacuee.

After several days or even weeks - time is a difficult concept when you are very young - people came to the hall to select children for billeting. I remember this well, it was traumatic. I was worried in case 1 was not selected and left alone in the hall. Eventually though, Mr and Mrs Marshall took me to their home in Cardonald where I remained throughout the war. During this time I received ten Red Cross messages from my mother who had stayed in Guernsey to look after her mother who was ailing. I attach a copy of one of those letters - it was the only contact I had with my mother in those five years. My father had joined the Army and he came to see me a couple of times.

When the war ended it was decided, for family reasons, that I should stay with Mr and Mrs Marshall, so when they moved to the Isle of Man I went with them. I finished my schooling in the Island and served an apprenticeship, before doing three years' National Service. Eventually I met and married a Castletown girl named Janet Cooil; Janet had an uncle named Harry Kinley who was a sea captain, and in due course I told him the story of my evacuation and the incident of the sweets. Imagine my amazement when he told me that the boat I had sailed on was the s.s. *Viking* commanded by Captain Bridson and that he was serving as the Second Officer on the boat that day, that the sweets and chocolates etc., had come from the lifeboats and that it could well have been his cabin I had travelled in. So there I was, all those years later, married to the niece of one of the officers of the ship that had evacuated me.

At the age of twenty-five I returned to Guernsey for the first time, to see my parents who had divorced at the end of the war. I had not seen my mother since I was seven - for eighteen years. It was a very emotional reunion. I met all the family and visited places I could hardly remember from my childhood days, but then I returned to my family in the Isle of Man where I have lived ever since."

Arthur Laine, Castletown, Isle of Man, April 2003

There are many stories recorded by those who were evacuated. They are recollections of childhood memories but I do not think that we can imagine the wrench that this must have been for parents who had to make such a difficult decision with so little time.

"At the time of the evacuation I was seven years old and my recollection of events is somewhat hazy. I believe we assembled at the Castel School about 6.30 p.m. on a lovely June evening only to be told to go home and return early next morning. We eventually departed by bus to the White Rock. 1,800 children and adults left for the security of the UK aboard the *Viking*.

The crossing was fairly uneventful. I can recall being given a bar of dark chocolate but spent most of my time on the deck being violently sick over the side. As we approached Weymouth I can just remember a plane passing over us.

On leaving the boat we were then transported by train to Bury Lanes. A small number, I think about fourteen of us, were under the care of Miss Florence Duchemin; we stayed at 20 Goldfinch Drive - double beds had four occupants, two at the top and two at the bottom.

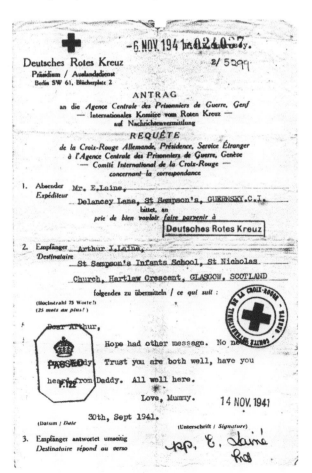

We were there for about three weeks then on to Plumley in Cheshire for three months, then finally to Ollerton in Cheshire for the next four years. The whole of this time I was accompanied by my younger brother Martyn who was just five years old and one of the youngest evacuees aboard the *Viking*. Finally I spent the last year in Oldham at the Boys' Intermediate School."

"After my usual after-school swim in Petit Bot Bay I was making my way home up the steep road when I was stopped by a man on a bicycle who told me to hurry back home because my mother was looking for me urgently. On my arrival at home I found that my mother had packed four little brown suitcases, one for each of her children. My brother aged 13, who was a student at Elizabeth College and my elder sister aged 14, who attended the Girls' Intermediate School (now the Grammar School) said goodbye and left almost immediately, my brother to join Elizabeth College which was moving to Buxton in Derbyshire and my elder sister to join her school which was moving to Rochdale in Lancashire. They both sailed that evening in the hold of a coal boat.

The following morning my mother, my younger sister Rose, then aged 7, and myself aged 11 left to walk the two miles to Le Gouffre Hotel, pushing a pram containing the suitcases. This hotel was the assembly point for the Forest Primary School, mothers with young children and elderly people wishing to leave Guernsey. We waited for the whole day only to be told to return the following day. That night, as I lay in bed, I could see the flashes and hear the gunfire in France.

The following morning we returned to Le Gouffre Hotel to wait again. This time my mother told me to go and push the pram over the cliff. I can still see the pram tumbling into the new bracken and gorse. Eventually we were driven in a bus to the harbour where we boarded the *Viking*. I remember overhearing that the ship had been slightly damaged by a bomb while evacuating soldiers from Dunkirk. My mother was given charge of eight other unaccompanied children from the Forest School of whom four were cousins of mine. We were allocated just enough space on one of the lower decks where we could all sit on the floor. I remember that my sister Rose was seasick and the only container that my mother could use was her felt hat! I had to clamber up to the deck to throw the hat overboard. I was rewarded for this effort by being given a hard biscuit, which had been retrieved from the emergency rations stored in a lifeboat, by one of the crew members.

We eventually arrived off Weymouth, where

*Survivors from the **Mona's Queen** [3] after the vessel was mined and sunk in Dunkirk on 29th June 1940. (Imperial War Museum)*

we had to wait off shore. We later disembarked and were taken to a cinema in Weymouth where we were given iced buns and tea. I then well remember seeing my very first railway train which took us all the way to Stockport where it was pouring with rain!"

"On the day we were supposed to travel (June 20th) we had gathered at Le Gouffre for the

Telephone No.: ABBEY 7711.

Any reply to this communication should quote the following reference

P.O 3385/S.T.N.1.

MINISTRY OF SHIPPING,
BERKELEY SQUARE HOUSE,
BERKELEY SQUARE,
LONDON, W.1.

4th June, 1940.

Gentlemen,

H.M.S. "KING ORRY"

I am directed by the Minister of Shipping to inform you that it was with great regret that he learned from the Admiralty of the loss of the above vessel It is not yet known what casualties have been caused and the list of Survivors has not yet been reported in detail, but in the event of any of the Officers who signed Admiralty agreement T.124 desiring to continue in Admiralty service, every endeavour will be made to secure them further employment in that service.

I am, Gentlemen,
Your obedient Servant,

The Isle of Man Steam Packet Co.Ltd.
Douglas,
Isle of Man.

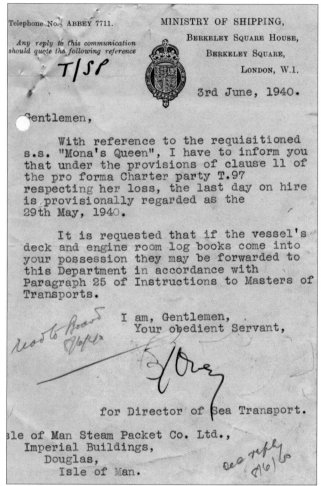

Telephone No.: ABBEY 7711.

Any reply to this communication should quote the following reference

T/SP

MINISTRY OF SHIPPING,
BERKELEY SQUARE HOUSE,
BERKELEY SQUARE,
LONDON, W.1.

3rd June, 1940.

Gentlemen,

With reference to the requisitioned s.s. "Mona's Queen", I have to inform you that under the provisions of clause 11 of the pro forma Charter party T.97 respecting her loss, the last day on hire is provisionally regarded as the 29th May, 1940.

It is requested that if the vessel's deck and engine room log books come into your possession they may be forwarded to this Department in accordance with Paragraph 25 of Instructions to Masters of Transports.

I am, Gentlemen,
Your obedient Servant,

for Director of Sea Transport.

Isle of Man Steam Packet Co. Ltd.,
Imperial Buildings,
Douglas,
Isle of Man.

journey to England. It was considered too dangerous to meet at the Forest School as it was very close to the airport. Mum had the care of nine or ten children, there were besides myself, sister Ruby, my cousin Margaret Dutchmin, three other cousins Leonard, Roselle and Gordon Robilliard plus Joan, Betty and Michael Sarre and another child whose name I cannot remember. The owner of a small shop at the Gouffre was giving away his stock of sweets, chocolates, crisps and fizzy drinks to the children who were taking advantage to get as much as they could, and eating as much of it as they could. Mum would not let us have any! She said it would make us seasick although she did stuff her handbag and pockets with as much as she could.

The ship did not arrive that day, and we all had to return to our homes. Dad had already gone to stay with friends in town. Our garden bordered on the airport and Mum decided it was safer to sleep downstairs, so we slept on the floor. We heard German planes overhead that night but nothing else happened. The following morning we were up early to walk to our gathering point at Le Gouffre; on our way Mr Vidamore the farmer was at his gate giving away milk and we enjoyed a cup of creamy

The **Lady of Mann** [1] arriving at Douglas to the north side of the Edward Pier in March 1946 to a very emotional return from war service prior to being prepared for civilian duties. I was present with my grandfather as an eight-year-old boy and remember the occasion vividly. (J.&M. Clarkson collection)

The **King Orry** [3] in her guise as an armed boarding vessel in the First World War. (Imperial War Museum)

fresh milk that he ladled out of the churn. A bus appeared. The driver stopped, and took us the rest of the way to Le Gouffre, saving us a walk carrying our luggage. When all the buses had arrived and loaded up we began our journey to the White Rock and the boat, our little group being among the last to go aboard the *Viking* (as I found out later) that would take us to England. We had to go below decks, and had to sit on the floor on a travel rug; there was not much room to move. It was not long before I was feeling sick, and as there was nothing else I had to use Mum's hat to be sick in. I cannot say if anyone else was seasick, as I was too busy being sorry for myself."

Those are just a few of the very personal recollections of those who were evacuated on that day in June 1940 which left such an indelible mark on the officers and crew of the *Viking*. She was not the only vessel involved in the evacuation of men, women and children as *Mona's Queen* [3] had evacuated civilians as well as troops from Ostend the previous month.

Information from the Record Office at Barrow shows that the *Manx Maid* [1] arrived at Barrow at the end of July 1940. She had worked between Liverpool and Douglas for the previous two months carrying aliens to the Island for internment. The vessel did not leave Barrow again until 10th November 1941 with Penmaenmawr as her destination after being fitted out as a radar training vessel.

The *Ben-my-Chree* [4] had returned briefly to Barrow from Channel service, leaving again on 21st April 1941 for Scottish waters. The *Lady of Mann* [1] arrived at Barrow in February 1942 from Invergordon where the vessel had been engaged trooping to Lerwick and Kirkwall, leaving again two months later for Invergordon for service to the Faeroes.

One of the many stories I heard from Captain Lyndhurst Callow sticks in my mind because of the way it was told and the peculiar circumstances of wartime Britain, and it also concerns the *Viking* on which he was a deck officer at the time -

"In 1944 the *Viking* was in dock at Gravesend to have a degaussing strip fitted together with the associated equipment as a countermeasure to the many magnetic mines that had been laid in the Straits of Dover which was the main area of operation for the vessel.

During this time in dock I had got to know the two WRNS girls on the gate to the dock quite well and was often invited into the gatehouse for a cup of tea and a chat. On one occasion I was enjoying a good conversation with them in the gatehouse which was a lot warmer than my cabin on board ship when one of the young ladies got up from her chair, grabbed my arm and rushed me outside. Somewhat surprised I didn't resist, in fact I was practically frog-marched round the back of the gatehouse into a brick pill box and thrown down on the ground with the other young lady following behind and throwing herself down on top!

I didn't know what to expect, then there was a loud explosion and the ground shook followed by the sound of breaking glass and debris falling. What the girls had heard which I hadn't was a V1 flying bomb or, as they were affectionately known, a 'doodlebug'. They would approach with a low droning noise at about 400 mph; as the fuel ran out they would make a stentorian noise and fall to earth, detonating on impact.

This was no exception as it landed in the dock area with disastrous results. My concern was for the ship and I immediately returned to the ship to find that it had been lifted bodily onto the quay wall, catching the belting and then falling back into the basin. There was a considerable amount of damage to the belting and the ship had suffered a huge amount of blast damage to cabin glazing and portholes on the side exposed to the explosion. There was also a considerable amount of shrapnel damage to the superstructure. Our return to sea was delayed while additional repairs were carried out."

It was a lucky escape as he could have been walking in the dock area to the ship when the explosion happened and been completely exposed.

It is a matter of record that the *Viking* "received damage on 27th June 1944 from a flying bomb which exploded in close proximity whilst in London Docks." After repair the ship resumed trooping duties from Southampton and Tilbury during August. With the end of hostilities in Europe the *Viking* arrived at Barrow, from London via Milford Haven on 23rd May 1945 having been released from Admiralty service, sailing for Liverpool on 13th June. The *Mona's Isle* [4] was also decommissioned at Barrow, leaving for Liverpool on 28th June 1945.

Some Steam Packet ships were in the Channel again in 1945 conveying troops back to demobilisation, sailing to ports in Belgium and Holland as well as France as the Channel was made secure and ports were cleared of obstructions. On cessation of hostilities in Europe ships were gradually returned to their owners. The Company got eight back: *Viking, Manxman* [1], *Mona's Isle* [4], *Snaefell* [4], *Manx Maid* [1], *Victoria, Ben-my-Chree* [4] and *Lady of Mann* [1].

Manxman was worn out at the end and considered uneconomic to repair; she never came back into service, being scrapped in 1949. New vessels were already in service and she was from a previous era. *Snaefell* [4] was in a similar condition and was withdrawn as soon as vessels came back from war service.

The *Victoria* and *Rushen Castle* were retained by the Company at the outbreak of war to operate the passenger service between Douglas and Liverpool. After *Victoria* was damaged by mines in the Mersey the service was transferred to Fleetwood. *Snaefell* [4] was released by the Ministry of War Transport to maintain the link between the UK and the Island and after repair *Victoria* took her place as an LSI transport vessel, performing with distinction at Arromanches with a Steam Packet crew.

The **King Orry** [3] *was not so fortunate and did not return from the Second World War - she is photographed in happier times in Scottish waters slowly approaching her berth at Ardrossan. (Bruce Peter collection)*

*Robert Lloyd's superb painting of **King Orry** (3) at the surrender of the German High Seas Fleet in November 1918, depicts her correctly at the centre of the flotilla of almost two hundred vessels. She was flanked by HMS **Blanche** and HMS **Boadecia** and acted as a signal repeating ship between HMS **Cardiff** at the head of the van and HMS **Castor** at the rear. She was also the only representative of the British mercantile fleet at the surrender.*

CHAPTER FIVE

Carrying the Goods

*What a wonderful picture taken from the Fort Anne Jetty looking towards the inner harbour at Douglas! The **Ben-my-Chree** [2] in her original 1875 form with two funnels is arriving at the Red Pier and it must be an important occasion judging by the top hats there to greet her. Was it her maiden voyage perhaps? (Manx National Heritage)*

The Steam Packet have carried mail and cargo to the Island since their inception. In fact the provision of a regular, reliable mail service was the reason for the formation of the Company. It has since that time provided an essential lifeline for the conveyance of all manner of goods except bulk cargoes to and from the Island. The first *Mona's Isle* carried no parcels on her inaugural sailing but is recorded as carrying the first parcel on her return journey from Liverpool for a Mrs Crellin. From then on parcel traffic appears on a regular basis with commodities such as hampers, cheeses and wine and more mundane items such as iron castings. Early in its life the Company was involved in intense competition with many other shipping companies, both local and from the rest of the British Isles. In an effort to secure as much of the available business as it could it fairly quickly established a regular

passenger and cargo service from Ramsey as well as Douglas. The Company purchased the business of their principal rival in that port and thereafter secured a monopoly. A cargo service was established at Castletown which was at the time of the inception of the Company the capital of the Island and the Company owned property on the Quay. The Governor of the Island resided there and it was a garrison town. Similarly a cargo shed was established next to the Fishermen's Shelter on the East Quay at Peel.

The early vessels were mainly passenger vessels but all carried mail and the Company advertised that they would 'carefully convey parcels for forwarding from Liverpool'. The vessels were not equipped to carry or handle loose cargo in any quantity but it did not stop them carrying items as large as small boats on deck. The first vessel to

Built initially as a paddle steamer and named **Mona's Isle** *[2], the vessel was converted to a twin-screw steamer in 1883 and was renamed* **Ellan Vannin**. *She is seen leaving Ramsey and is representative of the early vessels equipped for both passenger and cargo duties. Sadly the vessel was lost in the Mersey Channel in a storm in 1909 with all hands. (Stan Basnett collection)*

Cars were first brought to the Isle of Man in any quantity for the Gordon Bennett Trials of 1904. The vehicles were stowed wherever space could be found, often in precarious locations. (Stan Basnett collection)

appear with cargo-handling derricks was the *Snaefell* [2] built in 1875.

The *Mona's Isle* [2] ran as a paddle steamer for 23 years and then underwent a major rebuild in 1883 at the Naval Construction works at Barrow and emerged as a twin-screw vessel. The transformation was such that she was in effect a new vessel and was renamed *Ellan Vannin*; significantly she was fitted with hoisting derricks on both

masts serving two new cargo holds. She became the regular mail and cargo packet between Ramsey and Liverpool, continuing in service for almost 49 years.

The twin-screw *Fenella* [1] built in 1881 was primarily a cargo vessel with a limited passenger capacity of 504 with a view to carrying out winter relief passenger duty. She was fitted with cargo-handling gear on both masts serving holds forward and aft. One of the earliest twin-screw vessels built in the British Isles and the third longest-serving vessel owned by the Company, the vessel served on nearly all of the routes operated by the Steam Packet.

The *Peveril* [1] was built in 1884 and similarly equipped with two cargo holds - she was regularly used on the Ramsey station. The *Douglas* [3] was acquired second-hand and was also a dual-purpose vessel carrying two derricks on the foremast and a single derrick on the main. All these ships were ideally suited for the maintenance of

The **Mona's Isle** *[3] berthed at the Red Pier. It is half tide and calm in the late afternoon and the opportunity is being taken to dry the sails which all the early paddlers carried to supplement their speed in favourable conditions. (Manx National Heritage)*

The **Tyrconnel** *berthed at Peel, Isle of Man on the East Quay. She was engaged on the Northern Ireland/Isle of Man route carrying cargo only. (Stan Basnett collection)*

The Company did convey cargo to and from four of the Island's ports. Here is the **Cushag** *discharging cargo at the Quay in Castletown, the former capital of the Island and where the Company had a prestigious warehouse. (Collection of the late Captain Tom Corteen)*

Another view of Peel, this time the **Cushag** *is discharging at the East Quay. (Stan Basnett collection)*

the winter service and the *Douglas* was to be the mainstay during the First World War, supplying the Island with most of its essential food supplies.

From 1904 to 1908 the Island was host to the Gordon Bennett Motor Car Trials due to its peculiar situation with regard to its ability to legislate for closing roads and enabling these events to take place. The principal effect for the Company was the requirement for carrying these early automobiles to and from the Island. They were all craned on and off the ships and carried wherever they could be stowed on the deck, but they were exposed to the elements and there were complaints that damage had been caused to the electrical parts of some of the cars. The Company had to insure vehicles against loss.

This was to set the scene for the conveyance of cars for years to come. Motor events became very much a part of Island life and still are to the present time. Until the advent of the first car ferry *Manx Maid* [2] in 1962 all cars continued to be carried as deck cargo, usually on the

shelter deck of the later vessels. Even after the arrival of the first car ferries, cars and motorcycles continued to be carried on conventional ships particularly at Tourist Trophy time when every vessel was pressed into service. This is why the boat decks of the post-war passenger vessels had cut-away sections aft to facilitate loading vehicles to the shelter deck. Until the advent of *Peveril* [3] double-deck buses were conveyed to the Island across the forecastle of either the *Manxman* [2] or *King Orry* [4] which were provided with removable sections of bulwark to allow the buses to be driven off at Douglas, having usually been craned on at Liverpool.

The first purely cargo vessel was a small steam coaster purchased second-hand in 1920 and named *Cushag*. She was the first ship capable of carrying bulk cargo but the Company continued to carry break-bulk cargo and often split cargoes between different ports. Her size made her entirely suitable for Peel and Castletown.

The *Peveril* [2] was built in 1929 by Cammell Laird at

The **Conister** *[1] at the Steam Packet berth in Ramsey preparing for departure with last-minute loading and the Harbour Board grab dredger* **Mannin** *at work in the harbour. (Stan Basnett)*

The **Peveril** [2] approaching the Steam Crane Berth on the Battery Pier to discharge an engine for Peel power station. (Stan Basnett)

Ancient and modern together almost for the last time. It is New Year 1965 and the **Conister** [1] and **Peveril** [3] are in the inner harbour over the festive period. (Stan Basnett)

Birkenhead and was the first vessel built new for the Company and solely dedicated to the conveyance of cargo. She was originally designed without the four steam-operated derrick cranes which became the vessel's most distinguishing feature. They enabled the rapid discharge of general cargo but it was thought by some that they made the ship somewhat top-heavy and she was noted for her ability to roll in any sort of sea. The smell of hot oil and steam and the sound of the machinery of these steam cranes at work was unforgettable.

At the same time discharge of larger items as well as loose and bagged cargo over the side was also taking place using the ship's derricks. This was carried out by rigging two derricks yard-arm style or more correctly as a union purchase; one was secured plumb over the hold and one guyed out over the quay. The ends of the winch wires were shackled together and carried a swivel hook. The derricks were rigged on arrival by the crew but for cargo discharge winches were operated by stevedores who were employed by the Company. To see cargo discharged in this manner was poetry in motion – practice makes perfect!

The single-screw ship was propelled by a large triple-

January 1965 and the **Conister** [1] is towed away for scrap by Steele & Bennie's tug **Campaigner**. It was the end of an era, she was the last single-hatch coaster trading on the Irish Sea routes. (Stan Basnett)

You can almost smell this one! The **Conister** [1] is berthed at the Red Quay in Douglas ready to sail with a good head of steam and the last item is ready for loading – skins from the abattoir to be stacked in the open on the hatch and discharged as soon as possible at Birkenhead! (Stan Basnett)

*The **Peveril** [2] at the Tongue where she had been laid up awaiting disposal, now raising steam and about to leave in May 1964. (Stan Basnett)*

*The **Peveril** [2] in her prime, waiting for the tide in Liverpool Docks. (I.O.M.S.P.Co.)*

expansion engine with steam supplied from two boilers. The crew comprised the Captain, Mate and Second with up to six deckhands and below decks a Chief Engineer, Second Engineer, a greaser, a donkeyman and four firemen. No cook and they all had to do their own cooking.

Lyndhurst Callow when Captain of the *Peveril* [2] was once forced to turn back on a trip to Douglas because the weather in the Mersey was so bad he thought that to continue would risk capsizing. All I can say is that it must have really been bad! Notwithstanding she gave excellent service until 1964.

The *Conister* [1] formerly the *Abington* acquired in

1932 was similar in every respect to the *Cushag* and continued in service until 1965, becoming the last single-hatch steam cargo vessel operating in the Irish Sea. In her latter years she was the regular cargo vessel serving Ramsey although she would also be seen supplementing the Douglas service.

Facilities for the crew were virtually non-existent on these old steam coasters. The normal complement would be Skipper, Mate, Chief Engineer, Second Engineer, two deckhands and one fireman. The deckhands and fireman would live under the forepeak in basic accommodation with double bunks each side with a table and a bogie fire. The officers' accommodation was amidships with a small

*The **Peveril** [2] at the Tongue being de-commissioned ready for disposal. (Ian Collard)*

On one of her rare visits to Ramsey the **Fenella** *[3] causes a stir with many out to witness the event as she secures at the Steam Packet berth. (Stan Basnett)*

mess room below the wheelhouse. Watchkeeping was usually one man on/one man off with one officer and all hands to on arrival in or departure from port.

Fenella [3] was introduced in 1951 and was purpose-built for the Company by the Ailsa Shipbuilding Company of Troon. She incorporated many new features: perhaps the most notable was that she was the Company's first motor ship powered by a 7-cylinder British Polar engine. For the crew she set new standards in accommodation far beyond those even of the post-war passenger ships. All the accommodation was situated amidships on the shelter deck. Six Able Seamen were

accommodated in two-berth cabins on the starboard side next to the Second Officer with the Chief Officer forward below the bridge. On the port side a similar number of cabins accommodated two firemen greasers, the cook, Second and Third Engineers with the Chief Engineer on the port side below the bridge, with messing and cooking facilities central between the accommodation. This was a far cry from the post-war *King Orry* and her consorts where twelve deck crew were accommodated in one room in the forecastle. The twelve-man crew room was perpetuated on the passenger ships up to the car ferry *Ben-my-Chree* [5] with separate accommodation for deck crew

The **Fenella** *[3] arriving in Douglas with a following sea having been delayed by easterly gales. The freight service was maintained throughout the year by the cargo vessels in often desperate conditions. (Stan Basnett)*

The **Fenella** *[3] having arrived in easterly wind conditions is cautiously approaching the Office Berth to avoid being swept against the swing bridge. (Stan Basnett)*

carrying the goods

*The **Fenella** [3] in dry dock at Liverpool for survey. (H.B.Christiansen)*

*The **Fenella** [3] loading cattle in May 1960 at the Office Berth - they were always last on for discharge at the cattle lairage at Birkenhead. (Stan Basnett)*

*The January gales in 1966 and the **Fenella** [3] leaves Douglas for Liverpool. One of the ABs streams the log in matter-of-fact manner which is all in a day's work. He will probably go for his breakfast after that! (Stan Basnett)*

*The **Peveril** [2] also at Ramsey working the forward hatch with a part load for Ramsey. (Stan Basnett collection)*

and firemen all situated aft.

It was at this time that the old title of lamp-trimmer was replaced by Bosun or more correctly Boatswain for the leading Able Seaman of the deck crew. The lamp-trimmer was originally responsible for cleaning, filling and trimming the wick of all the lamps on board, not only in the accommodation but principally the navigation lights which was of course a responsible job. The use of paraffin lamps reduced with the introduction of electric lighting especially for navigation purposes but even as late as 1970 they were used in the crew accommodation after 5 p.m. when the generators were shut down.

Watchkeeping on the larger cargo ships was different from the passenger vessels but the deck crew were still split into a forward watch and an aft watch. On the *Fenella* [3] it was usual for one helmsman and one officer to be on watch at a time. The custom of the forward watch being on during passage from Douglas to the Mersey and the aft watch from Liverpool to Douglas was applied on the cargo vessels. Terms of engagement under Articles were for the crew to work eight hours in eleven which allowed

*During easterly gales the normal cargo berth became untenable and here the **Fenella** [3] has moved to the inner harbour to complete her discharge. (Stan Basnett)*

*The **Peveril** [3] assisting in the discharge of double-deck buses carried as deck cargo. A bus from the starboard side is being transferred to the opposite side within range of the 25-ton steam crane on the Battery Pier. (Stan Basnett)*

*The **Peveril** [3] as originally built with self-discharge cranes is being warped onto the Office Berth for discharge. (Stan Basnett)*

A stunning evening view of the **Fenella** [3] *in Coburg Dock. (Ian Collard)*

LK135

*The **King Orry [4]** arriving at Douglas with a bus for the IOM Road Services. Before the arrival of the **Peveril [3]** double-deck buses were carried across the foredeck of either the **King Orry [4]** or the **Manxman [2]**, both vessels having removable rails to allow buses to be driven off at the Edward Pier. (Stan Basnett)*

*An AEC Regent Mk IV sits on the foredeck of the **King Orry [4]** waiting for the exact time to be off-loaded. (Stan Basnett)*

With the operation complete the bus is almost off the ship, care being taken with the rear overhang of the bus to ensure that the foredeck of the ship and the pier are level. (Stan Basnett)

The timing for driving the bus off the ship was crucial. Four minutes were all that were available for the operation to be successfully carried out either on the rise or fall of the tide when deck and pier were almost level. (Stan Basnett)

*The **Peveril** [3], now converted for unitised cargo handling using standard containers, being loaded by the Butters 28-ton derrick crane. (Stan Basnett)*

*The **Peveril** [3] underway with vehicles stowed on the hatch covers, the method used before the advent of RoRo services. (Stan Basnett)*

flexibility having regard to the longer passage times and vagaries of weather.

The deck layout of the *Fenella* [3] was unusual: the main deck sometimes described as an orlop deck was carried forward full length as a 'tween deck. It had a rear hatch and a forward hatch and coamings. A shelter deck was carried from midships forward and this was also fitted with a hatch and coaming immediately above the lower one - loose cargo could be carried on this deck as well as within the hold. Demountable cattle pens for 80 to 100 animals were also situated on the main deck. Usually there were four cattle to a pen or sixteen sheep although horses were partitioned off to accommodate one animal to a pen.

As with any vessels carrying livestock from the Island these were discharged at Woodside Lairage, Birkenhead. After discharge and before entering Coburg Dock for normal discharge the pens would be stowed and the crew required to wash down and scrub the decks. Cargo vessels would normally enter the Liverpool dock system through the Brunswick entrance although occasionally they would

use the Herculaneum entrance which would necessitate navigating through the dock system. The most unpopular cargo without doubt was the carriage of hides which was always the last item to be delivered to the ship from the abattoir and stowed as deck cargo.

The *Peveril* [3] was built at Troon in 1963 to replace *Peveril* [2], and although built on a unitised format she carried two Stothert & Pitt cranes for self-discharge and continued the policy of handling break-bulk cargo. She also had much improved crew accommodation with two-man cabins for the crew and the usual officers' cabins. The *Ramsey* was built in the same yard in 1964 to replace the *Conister* [1].

During 1972 the Steam Packet after much deliberation made the decision, forced on them by modern trends, to abandon their break-bulk cargo-handling policy and convert to full containerisation. It had been creeping in anyway but the vessels and the warehouse area were not geared to handle this type of traffic.

The former Imperial Hotel had by this time been

*The **Ramsey** in Coburg Dock which was the Steam Packet break-bulk cargo discharge location in Liverpool. Now no more and part of the dockland development. (Ian Collard)*

Mail was the reason for the Company's formation in 1830 and collection from the packet boat has changed over the years from collection by hand cart to collection by vans. In this 1961 photograph a single van waits for a winter arrival from Liverpool. (Stan Basnett)

Even with the advent of the car ferries the mail was still carried off the ship by the crew and loaded into Post Office vans which awaited the arrival of the daily sailing from Liverpool. (Ferry Publications Library)

Company had purchased the ship and in December she was renamed *Conister* (2), becoming the second vessel to bear the name. The two ships were destined to run an alternate daily service.

There was an interesting period of charter whenever either of these vessels went for annual overhaul. Amongst the vessels used were the *Lune Fisher*, *Dorset Coast* and *Mountcrest*.

In June 1981 the Steam Packet commenced their Ro-Ro service with the *N.F.Jaguar* initially on bareboat charter and later purchased by the Company, becoming *Peveril* [4] for a freight-only service with limited driver accommodation. *Mona's Isle* [6] ex *Free Enterprise* [3] was to provide the first fully-integrated Ro-Ro service but she arrived at an unfortunate time in the Company's history and with problems over the ship herself and the port facilities at Liverpool she was quickly replaced by the *Antrim Princess* on charter, later to become *Tynwald* [6]. This ship provided good service but she was an old vessel and following new requirements for safety at sea in the wake of the Zeebrugge disaster it was decided that a replacement was a pressing need.

Eventually suitable second-hand tonnage was found in the form of the Sealink vessel *Channel Entente*. After completing successful berthing trials at Douglas on 11th January 1990 she was acquired by the Company, entering service the following month. Initially she ran under her Sealink name but by the end of the year, and following modifications including the provision of a side-loading door for use at Liverpool, she was renamed *King Orry* [5]. She was to give excellent service until replaced by the *Ben-my-Chree* [6] in 1998.

demolished and work started in the early part of 1972 on the erection of a 28-ton capacity Butters electrically operated derrick crane for handling containers. By July the crane was in service and the *Peveril* [3] was taken out of service and sent to Troon for conversion to full unitised container traffic; the main visible outward sign on her return was the removal of the two cargo-handling cranes. During the time of the conversion two vessels from the Ramsey Steamship Company were chartered to carry the cargo.

The *Fenella* [3] proved almost impossible to use with container traffic and was disposed of in December 1972. The following year the *Spaniel* was chartered to assist in dealing with the increased traffic; by November the

*It was only with the arrival of the first ro-ro vessels that things started to change and mail started to arrive in containers, to be sorted in a rented part of the old parcels shed. Here is the first such vessel **Mona's Isle** [6] being assisted onto her berth by the tug **Salisbury**. (Stan Basnett)*

A view along the main car deck of the **Mona's Isle** [6] showing the mezzanine deck which could be raised or lowered depending on the vehicles being carried. The pattern of cargo handling had now changed for ever. (Stan Basnett)

The **Belard**, a freight-only ro-ro vessel owned for a short while by the Company, is berthed at the new King Edward Pier linkspan. (Stan Basnett)

Eventually as a consort to the **King Orry** [5], the **Peveril** [4] ran an exclusive freight-only service to Heysham with limited overnight driver accommodation and became the mainstay of the cargo operation for sixteen years, having initially run from Liverpool Hornby Dock. (Miles Cowsill)

CHARTERED CARGO VESSELS POST WORLD WAR TWO:

ss Seaville	mv Ben Vooar
ss Sprayville	mv Linda
ss Monksville	mv Daunt Rock
ss Avanville	mv Ben Veen
mv Saga Moon	mv Ben Varrey
mv European Mariner	mv Spaniel
mv River Lune	mv Lune Fisher
mv Belard	mv Dorset Coast
mv NF Jaguar	mv Stena Sailer
mv Lion	mv Moondance
mv East Express	mv CFF Seine
mv Clipper Ranger	mv Stena Caledonia
mv Phocine	mv Triumph
mv Merchant Brilliant	mv West Express
mv Helliar	mv Mountcrest
mv Mette Ris	mv Dart 1
mv Hoburgen	mv Riverdance

The **King Orry** [5], the ro-pax vessel which gave excellent service for the Company until the arrival of the **Ben-my-Chree** [6], inward bound to Liverpool where she offered a private vehicle and small van-only service, due to weight limitations at Liverpool Landing Stage. (Ian Collard)

Between 1950 and 1951 J.S.Monk Ltd had three of their vessels on charter to the Steam Packet Co. – and the **Seaville** *was one of them. The vessel collided with a hopper barge in the Mersey near Q15 buoy whilst on charter. Eleven of the twelve -man crew were rescued by the Liverpool Pilot Boat. (Billy Stowell collection)*

The **Avanville** *was another of J.S Monk's coasters that the Steam Packet Co. chartered and is seen discharging at the Steam Packet's cargo berth in 1950. The other vessel in the picture is the IoM Harbour Board's workboat* **Sirdar***. (Dick Clague collection)*

The **Linda** photographed between the piers leaving Douglas with a full cargo of containers while on charter during January 1980. (Stan Basnett)

The **Dorset Coast** on charter during November and December 1975. (Stan Basnett)

The **Hoburgen** owned by Rederi AB Gotland was chartered to cover for the **Ben-my-Chree** [6] whilst she was undergoing her refit in 2004. (Stan Basnett)

The **Spaniel** of Coast Lines on charter between July and October 1973 before being purchased by the Company to become the **Conister** [2]. (Stan Basnett)

The **Dart 1** at the Edward Pier linkspan on charter to cover for the **Ben-my-Chree's** refit in 2000. (Stan Basnett)

The **Saga Moon** on short-term charter in June 1993 departing from Douglas. (Stan Basnett)

*Ramsey Steamship Co. Ltd. have provided charter vessels as required and here the **Ben Vooar** (3) is on charter in January 1968 handling break bulk cargo. (Stan Basnett)*

*The **Daunt Rock** photographed on 27th August 1979 at the Steam Packet cargo berth by this time converted for container traffic, was on charter covering for **Peveril** (3) during the period of her annual survey. (Stan Basnett)*

The **Lune Fisher** was chartered by the Company on three separate occasions in 1973, 1974 and 1976. (Stan Basnett)

The **River Lune** was chartered for freight duty during TT Week 2005 to allow the **Ben-my-Chree** [6] to carry more motorcycles and support vehicles and her full complement of passengers. (Stan Basnett)

The **Mette Riis** was chartered during a strike by seamen and provided a limited service between Mostyn and Douglas. (Stan Basnett)

The **Riverdance** was chartered in May 2002 at short notice to cover for the **Ben-my-Chree** [6] when she had to dry-dock for emergency work to be undertaken. (Stan Basnett)

The **European Mariner** on charter from 21st January to 11th February 2002 providing additional freight capacity during the **Ben-my-Chree's** refit. (Stan Basnett)

*During the **Ben-my-Chree**'s 2008 refit Seatruck's freighter **Triumph** was chartered to provide freight cover later than originally planned due to commitments elsewhere. This has become an increasing problem for the company with less suitable tonnage available for charter to meet length restrictions at both Heysham and Douglas. (Stan Basnett)*

*The **East Express** was chartered in 2008 to handle additional freight generated by the TT motorcycle events. Here we see the freighter making its approach to Douglas on 9th June 2008 having just taken on the Douglas harbour pilot. (Stan Basnett)*

*Mention of the additional traffic generated as a result of the TT motorcycle festival saw **Stena Caledonia** first visiting the Island in June 2007. She was one of a number of vessels chartered to relieve the pressure on the **Ben-my-Chree** (6), which is inward bound to Douglas in this photograph. (Miles Cowsill)*

*To provide additional capacity for passengers coming to the Island from Northern Ireland for the festival the Steam Packet have chartered P&O's fast craft **Express** to run a special service from Larne to Douglas and return at the beginning and end of the festival period. (Stan Basnett)*

CHAPTER SIX

Away from Home

Until the formation of the Steam Packet Company in 1830, most services to the Isle of Man had been provided by vessels trading either between Cumbrian ports and Ireland, where the livestock trade underpinned services, or the North/South routes between the Mersey and the Clyde. Passenger and freight traffic for western Scotland could not easily be moved overland from the north of England. The Isle of Man lay in the path of both these traffic routes, and so little deviation was required for ships to call in at Manx ports – when there was enough business to justify it. Once the Steam Packet Company were established on the Liverpool route there was less incentive for passing ships to continue their Manx calls, so that very early in the Company's history services to ports other than Liverpool were developed.

The coming of the railways later in the 19th century facilitated the movement of large numbers of passengers between the mill towns and cities of the north of England and coastal ports and resorts. It was also now both possible and practicable to charter a ship for a works outing and there were many regular charters over the years. Although the Liverpool-Manchester Railway opened in 1830 it was 1857, the same year that the original Prince's Landing Stage opened, before there was a rail link to London. Fleetwood was linked by rail to Preston from 1840 onwards. This had the effect of concentrating shipping services through those ports which were rail-connected and services from other ports dwindled, particularly as ships became larger. The other development was that of

*The **Lady of Mann** (1) alongside the Liverpool berth on the south side of Ramsey Queen's Pier in July 1968 on her morning sailing to Ardrossan. This berth was usually used when the wind was from the east, which caused difficulties when using the berthing head of the pier. (Stan Basnett)*

*Yes, the car ferries did occasionally call at Ramsey Queen's Pier on passage to Belfast. The year is still 1968 and the **Ben-my-Chree** [5] is coming up to the pier head. (Stan Basnett)*

*There was a time when the Steam Packet ran a service from Ramsey to Whitehaven prior to the First World War. Here we see the **Mona** (3) sometime between 1903 and 1909 departing from Ramsey harbour, which was tidal. (T. Midwood - Stan Basnett collection)*

*The **Lady of Mann** [2] secured alongside Ramsey South Pier on Sunday 19th May 1991 at the berth once regularly used by the Company's passenger vessels. (Stan Basnett)*

*The **Mona's Isle** [5] diverted to Peel on 17th February 1966. The wind is from the south east which is why the vessel has approached bow-in to avoid the wind getting the wrong side and blowing her off the pier. If that happened it would necessitate moving astern into the bay and making a second approach. (Stan Basnett)*

*January is noted around the Island for gales from the easterly quadrant and 1970 was exceptional. The **Snaefell** [5] has been diverted to Peel as Douglas was untenable in such conditions. The vessel dominates the pier and entry to the harbour demanded expert seamanship and local knowledge. (Stan Basnett)*

*The **Mona's Isle** [5] approaches Llandudno which like all landing piers required care and local knowledge because of the set of the tides and the movement of sand bars around such structures. (Ian Collard)*

*Back to January 1970 again as the **Snaefell** [5] approaches Peel breakwater in a blizzard on a second attempt. In a full easterly gale, before the advent of bow thrusters, the trick was to set the stern down on the pier and let the wind carry the bow in, checking with the port anchor as necessary. (Stan Basnett)*

The **Lady of Mann** (2) off the beaten track at Whitehaven in 1989 with a special pre-season trip from the Island. (Bryan Kennedy)

Steam Packet ships were not always laid up at Birkenhead or Barrow. In this photograph we see the **Manxman** (2) at Govan on 20th April 1980 for dry docking prior to the start of the 1980 season. (Lawrence Macduff)

piers – any sizeable Victorian resort wanted to have its own pier – and if it had a pier it usually wanted to have excursion steamers operating from it as well. Blackpool North Pier had a rather basic steamer jetty from 1867 and Llandudno Pier opened in 1878, although Bangor in the Menai Straits was not to open until nearly twenty years later. Whilst summer excursions ran from various Lancashire and North Wales piers to the Island, this was a trade in which, for the most part, the Steam Packet vessels were too large or deep-draughted – or otherwise employed. The only piers the Company have used regularly are Llandudno (but mainly between 1963 and 1982) and Queen's Pier, Ramsey en route from Douglas to Belfast or Ardrossan (1886 and 1970).

Although the railway companies were active in Irish Sea shipping, it was only the Midland Railway – initially through its investment in the Barrow Steam Navigation Company - which took responsibility for Isle of Man services from 1868, but later in its own right from Heysham, that ran its own services to the Island, from 1905. These passed to the London, Midland & Scottish Railway (LMS) in 1923, but only until 1927, after which

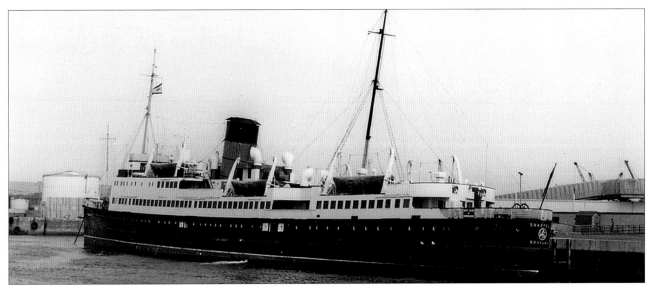

During the summer season the Steam Packet ran a regular service between Douglas and Ardrossan calling at Ramsey Queen's Pier. Here the **Snaefell** (5) is photographed at Ardrossan on 15th July 1977 one month before she finished. (Lawrence Macduff)

*Christmas 1978 and two car ferries are at Peel, the **Mona's Queen** [5] at the breakwater and the **Lady of Mann** [2] at anchor in the bay due again to sustained easterly gales closing Douglas Harbour over the holiday period. (Stan Basnett)*

*The **Mona** [4] high and dry in Ramsey Harbour at the berth used by the deeper-draught vessels and the same one used by the **Lady of Mann** [2] on her 1991 visit. (Stan Basnett collection)*

the Steam Packet Company took over the service. Even then the railways were keen to ensure that there were enough ships running to uplift the increasing numbers of excursionists which they conveyed to the ports of Fleetwood and Heysham.

There have also been great events to celebrate – wonders and spectacles which excursionists could visit by the shipload. The Company's first recorded excursion in 1830, taken by the new *Mona's Isle,* was to view Thomas Telford's Menai Bridge which had only opened four years earlier and was at that time by far the largest suspension bridge in the world.

These various influences led to a much greater variety of destinations being served at different times than would be economic today, when the traveller merely has to drive

*The **Snaefell** [2] at Peel. I have no idea who took the photograph which for many years was pinned to the door of the compressor house in Poortown Quarry before being retrieved by me! (Stan Basnett collection)*

*On Saturday 30th June 1990 the **Mona's Queen** [5] called at Port St Mary breakwater during a special cruise to Port St Mary and the Calf of Man to commemorate the 160th Anniversary of the Company. (Stan Basnett)*

The **Ben-my-Chree** [6] on the 175th Anniversary Commemorative Round the Island cruise passing behind Port St Mary breakwater. (Barbara O'Friel)

The 1989 – 1990 Whitbread Round the World Race saw the **Mona's Queen** (5) chartered by the French Post Office at Southampton in support of their yacht La Poste. (John Hendy)

to the port from which the ferry happens to operate. Today's ferry industry relies on vehicles and freight much more than foot passengers for its viability: ships can only be viable if worked intensively, and so the days of the spare ship, available for duties "away from home", are disappearing fast.

SCOTTISH ROUTES

With the delivery of their second ship – the *Mona* – in 1832, a second route, from Whitehaven to Dublin via Douglas, was instituted as well as excursions to Kirkcudbright and Garlieston in south west Scotland. Kirkcudbright sailings have since been rare, with an excursion to the Island on which the *Fenella* [1] and the *Ellan Vannin* were used in 1902 possibly being the last. Garlieston enjoyed a period of weekly Steam Packet summer services between 1866 and 1879 and through tickets by connecting train to Glasgow were offered in 1878 and 1879. Thereafter there were only excursions although they were particularly popular during the late 1890s when two or three trips might be offered in each of the peak summer months - usually using the *King Orry* [2] or *Tynwald* [3]. The *Victoria* was certainly at Garlieston as late as July 1953.

Stranraer had occasional calls at the end of the 19th century, some voyages also involving calls at Garlieston, with excursion passengers being offered the opportunity

The **King Orry** (4) presents a classic profile of the post-war sister ships built by Cammell Laird as she leaves Ardrossan on 14th July 1974 bound for Douglas with the afternoon sailing. (Lawrence Macduff)

The **Snaefell** [5] *in Scottish waters leaving Ardrossan. (Bruce Peter collection)*

to travel overland between the two ports. In 1937 the *Peel Castle* was chartered by the Territorial Army for a trip to Ramsey from Stranraer. In the 1960s there were a number of Stranraer Town Band charters to the Island, some of which used Steam Packet vessels, although in other years Sealink ships operated. In 1986 the Ardrossan – Isle of Man service was transferred to Stranraer, with the usual vessel being the *Mona's Queen* [5], but this was

withdrawn at the end of its second season.

The development of Clyde services certainly goes back much further than A.W. Moore suggests in his 1904 History of the Company – when he described them as being of "recent" origin. In the early days the custom was to advertise "Glasgow Services" although the arrival time given was almost certainly that of the train. The earliest reference to a Clyde sailing was an excursion to Ardrossan

The **Manxman** [1] *gliding down the Firth of Clyde bound for Douglas. (Bruce Peter collection)*

*Still in Scottish waters and again at Ardrossan, the **Tynwald** [4] approaches the harbour. This side-on view shows the profile of the pre-war sisters from which the post-war developments can be easily compared. From an appearance point of view the most controversial feature was without doubt the funnel top and bands constructed parallel to the waterline. (Bruce Peter collection)*

in 1845 although the port was not regularly advertised until the 1890s. Glasgow sailings were advertised as early as 1868, although the fortnightly service that season was withdrawn at the end of June. A couple of years later a weekly service was reduced to fortnightly by mid-July. The Company's earliest ships were all Clyde-built and in 1865 and 1869 the *Tynwald* [1] and *Tynwald* [2] returned to Greenock for boiler inspections, with the sailings being advertised to carry passengers. In 1874 separate monthly services were offered to Glasgow and Greenock. When regular Ardrossan services started in the 1890s, Greenock calls were no longer being advertised although Glasgow was advertised at least until 1907, in some cases with calls at Ardrossan en route. It was the custom to show train connections to Glasgow and the quickest timings from

city centre to Douglas could usually be achieved by leaving Glasgow by train rather than ship. Apart from wartime interruptions, Ardrossan summer services continued until 25th August 1985 although, after the closure of the replacement service via Stranraer, the Caledonian MacBrayne vessel *Claymore* offered a limited service on the route between 1994 and 1997. Greenock was used as a diversion port if ships could not enter Ardrossan in bad weather, with the last call on that basis probably being made by the *Manx Maid* [2] in 1980.

Although not offering regular services, Steam Packet vessels have operated excursion and charter sailings to other Clyde ports. William Gray Carpets certainly chartered the *Tynwald* [3] from Ayr to Douglas as early as 1914. Between 1967 and 1975 there were nine sailings

*The **Mona's Isle** [6] leaving the Grand Harbour of Malta en route for service with the Isle of Man Steam Packet Company. (The late Captain Vernon Kinley)*

*A lovely shot of the **King Orry** [3] in a fresh breeze inward bound in the Firth of Clyde. (Bruce Peter collection)*

The **Lady of Mann** (2) returns to her birthplace after 29 years as part of the Isle of Man Steam Packet Company's 175th Anniversary celebrations on 20th May 2005. (Miles Cowsill)

The **Claymore** is pictured here arriving at Douglas from Ardrossan. (Miles Cowsill)

between Ayr and either Belfast or Larne. Rothesay and Dunoon have only seen occasional visits by Steam Packet vessels, with the *Ben-my-Chree* [3] running a shareholder excursion to Dunoon in 1909 and the *Tynwald* [5] grounding there on a charter in 1952. There were two calls (a week apart) at Rothesay in July 1969. Charters of Manx vessels to Scottish shipping companies have been rare, but in November 1861 the *Douglas* [1] - which in 1864 was commissioned as the USS *Gettysburg* - ran on the Ardrossan/Belfast service for three weeks, and almost a hundred years later the *Manxman* [2] covered for the *Royal Ulsterman* on the same route.

ENGLISH ROUTES

Although the Steam Packet Company were involved in the Whitehaven route from 1832 onwards, they certainly did not have a monopoly and a number of other

The car ferry **Lady of Mann** [2] leaves the Irish port of Dun Laoghaire for Douglas in March 1990. (Gordon Hislip)

The **Tynwald** [3] at Garlieston, in Wigtown Bay, Galloway almost certainly in 1920 when occasional sailings were resumed after the First World War. (Stan Basnett collection)

The **Mona's Queen** [4] leaves Ardrossan bound for Douglas, the bow rope not yet taken up. (Bruce Peter collection)

*The **Tynwald** [5] at the north end of Liverpool Landing Stage when it was still in use as a trans-atlantic terminal. (McRoberts collection)*

companies such as the North British Rail & Steam Packet Company served both Silloth and Whitehaven for nearly forty years. The combination of competition and inadequate dredging at Whitehaven meant that Steam Packet interest in the route waxed and waned and it appears they operated very few services between 1850 and 1870 when Ramsey - Whitehaven services operated – but by June 1878 a daily service was offered between the two ports. By the late 1880s depth of water was a problem again and services were much reduced after 1888, ceasing completely with the outbreak of war in 1914. Regular services to Whitehaven never resumed thereafter, although the *Lady of Mann* [2] provided an annual excursion sailing for several years up to 2005.

In 1929 only a short-lived summer service was provided from Ramsey to Workington. There were several annual charters from Workington to Douglas between 1946 and 1954, worked by the *Victoria, Mona's Queen* [4] and *Tynwald* [5].

The Steam Packet have not run Barrow services although the *Douglas* [2] was chartered to Little & Co. for several months during the winter of 1887/88 to run four trips a week on their Barrow-Belfast service. Manx services were provided by the Barrow Steam Navigation Company for nearly forty years from 1868 and so the Steam Packet never offered regular services there, although the *Tynwald* [2] was chartered to the Barrow Company in 1885 to enable their regular steamer to go to the assistance of another which had run aground. Special sailings were run in 1930 and 1936 to take the Steam Packet Directors and Company guests to Barrow for the launch of the *Lady of Mann* [1] and the *Fenella* [2] and *Tynwald* [4]. In September 1992 the *Lady of Mann* [2] was chartered to port owners Associated British Ports (ABP) to mark the 125th Anniversary of the opening of the Port of Barrow.

*By way of a contrast here is a view of Fleetwood with the **Manxman** [2] present on a day trip from Douglas. (Stan Basnett)*

*The **Lady of Mann** [2] arriving at Heysham on 12th June 2005 in her last year in service. (Martin Edmundson)*

The Midland Railway opened the port of Heysham in 1904 and its own Isle of Man services the next year. After the re-organisation of the railways in 1923, the service was taken over by the newly-formed LMS, who then transferred it, with two ships, to the Steam Packet Company with a ten-year service level agreement from 1928. With the Steam Packet already having their own Fleetwood service, the route played second fiddle to Fleetwood after the Second World War, only resuming with a very limited service between 1953 and 1974. It was only in 1985, following the merger with the Sealink-Manx Line, that the Steam Packet again provided services from Heysham.

Fleetwood Steam Packet summer services only got onto a firm footing from 1876 although there were limited services in the 1840s and 1855, as well as joint services with Kemp & Co. from 1847 to 1851 and in 1866 and 1867. The main Liverpool service was transferred to Fleetwood during the Second World War but in 1946 the service reverted to seasonal operation. Services ceased at the end of the 1961 season when funds could not be found to repair the berth. They re-started ten years later but by 1986 the Steam Packet Company were seeking to concentrate their services on Heysham and the service looked lost until ABP, the port owner, stepped in and chartered the *Mona's Queen* [5] to operate a limited number of "Fun Boat" sailings in 1986. Following this the port returned to the timetable until 1997, although by then services were only weekly except for a short period in September/October 1996 when sailings were provided to Dublin and the Island, but from 1998 onwards only one

or two excursion sailings have been provided by the *Lady of Mann* [2] each summer.

It was only in 1929 that the Steam Packet Company ran services from Blackpool Pier but the draught of the *Tynwald* [3] proved problematic and the experiment was never repeated. Back in 1905 the two local companies had merged and asked the Manx company to take over their routes to Liverpool, Llandudno and Douglas so that they could concentrate on local excursions, but the Steam Packet suggested that passengers wishing to visit the Island should travel via Fleetwood!

*The **Mona's Queen** [2] arriving at Whitehaven on the Ramsey-Whitehaven service. (Steam Packet collection)*

*The **SeaCat Isle of Man** at Berth 49, Dublin Port in August 1995. (Gordon Hislip)*

Liverpool was the Company's main destination from August 1830 to the end of March 1985 – both for cargo and passenger traffic. In 1834 daily services operated in summer (but not on Sundays) and in 1848 a Liverpool-Ramsey weekly service started. It was not until 1879 that there was a daily service all the year round. The original services ran to St George's Dock, on the site of which the Liver Building now stands. There were no locks and so the ship had to wait for the tide to enter the dock – or put passengers ashore using small boats. It was not until 1857 that the first landing stage was built, enabling passengers to embark at all states of the tide. This was replaced in 1874 by a new stage which promptly caught fire and it was not until 1876 that things were back to normal. Apart from the war period between Christmas 1940 and Spring 1946 when operations were transferred to Fleetwood, the

*A splendid photograph of **SuperSeaCat Two** in the Mersey in choppy conditions. (Ian Collard)*

away from home

*The **Manx Maid** [2] at Liverpool Landing Stage with the classic Liverpool Pier Head buildings presenting the backdrop. (Stan Basnett)*

landing stage at Liverpool Pier Head has provided the berth for the Company's Liverpool operations. By 1970 the condition of this stage was so poor that a replacement was clearly required, although it was not until Summer 1977 that the replacement facility became operational. A total £2.75 million was provided by the Manx Government towards the cost of the new stage, a sum which the Company had to repay over the next twenty-five years. There appears to have been no discussion about a modified design to handle stern-loading ships, the Company by then having invested in four side-loading car ferries. Once the economic necessity of Ro-Ro passenger operation became apparent only seven years later the main service was switched to Heysham, when the Company merged with Sealink-Manx Line.

The lack of Liverpool services proved unpopular and

*The **Lady of Mann** [2] underway in the River Mersey bound for Douglas. (Ian Collard)*

*The **Manxman** [2] at Holyhead on 29th May 1978 on an educational cruise from the Island. (Stan Basnett)*

*The **SuperSeaCat Two** at Liverpool Landing Stage at night awaiting departure. (Ian Collard)*

*The **Lady of Mann** [2] at Barrow on the occasion of the 175th Anniversary celebratory trips to ports with links to the Company through shipbuilding and repair. (Stan Basnett)*

*A wonderfully atmospheric photograph full of interesting detail for anyone interested in industrial archaeology as the **Peel Castle** enters dry dock at Cammell Laird, Birkenhead with ropes in place to ensure the correct location over the blocks. (Merseyside Maritime Museum/McRoberts collection)*

*The **Mona's Isle** [5] leaving Preston. (J. & M. Clarkson)*

On board the **Lady of Mann** [2] travelling up the Manchester Ship Canal for annual survey at Pomona dry dock, Salford in March 1978. (Stan Basnett)

On board the **Manxman** [2] turned and navigating astern to Belfast. (Stan Basnett)

by Summer 1986 a twice-weekly service was re-introduced - better than nothing but a mere shadow of the twice-daily service previously provided. Through the 1990s services built up again, reaching a level of six per week in Summer 1994 when the *SeaCat Isle of Man* was introduced. She discharged vehicles over a pontoon ramp, moored alongside the landing stage, which has been used by fast craft in all subsequent summers. By Summer 2000 Liverpool was again having a twice-daily fast craft service to the Isle of Man, with the traditional four-hour journey time reduced to 2.5 hours, and, although winter services were confined to weekends, Liverpool had regained its position as the main passenger port for the Isle of Man.

NORTH WALES

Llandudno Pier opened in 1877 and there seems to have been a one-off excursion from Douglas to view it in 1878. By the time the Company offered a "new service" in 1906 others, including the Barrow Steam Navigation Company, had been on the route for more than ten years. The "new service" was not a success and after a couple of

The **Lady of Mann** [2] arriving light ship at Warrenpoint in June 2000 to take an excursion sailing to Douglas. (Dick Clague)

*The **Mona's Queen** (5) inward bound to Dublin from Douglas in 1989. (Gordon Hislip)*

calls in July 1907 the Company left the route alone save for a flurry of excursions in 1930. Between 1963 and 1982 the Company stepped in first on the Liverpool-Llandudno and later the Douglas-Llandudno route following the

demise of the Liverpool & North Wales Steamship Co. From 1997 onwards the *Lady of Mann* [2] again provided a small number of excursion opportunities each summer.

There were day trips recorded to Bangor in 1866 and 1867. The pier was opened in 1896 and there were further occasional sailings between 1898 and 1901 by the *King Orry* [2], *Tynwald* [3] and *Snaefell* [2]. Bangor was however shown as an excursion destination in the Company's literature as late as 1909. Vessels proceeding to Menai Bridge would often call at Beaumaris and Bangor en route and there were certainly some Steam Packet sailings up the Straits at this period – if only evidenced by the grounding of the *Fenella* [1] in 1884. For the most part such sailings as there have been from the Straits to the Island were provided by the Liverpool & North Wales

*The **Tynwald** [5] berthed at the North Wall, Dublin. (Ian Collard)*

*The **Mona's Isle** [5] and **Tynwald** [5] at Llandudno. (Ian Collard)*

The **King Orry** (5) *departing from Dublin for Douglas on one of her Christmas crossings during 1996. (Gordon Hislip)*

Steamship Company not the Steam Packet whose vessels, in more recent years, would have been too big for the Straits. In August 1890 the *Mona's Isle* [3] was chartered by Lever Bros. to Beaumaris, but this sailing was almost certainly from Liverpool.

The final Welsh route was Holyhead. The first recorded visit by a Steam Packet vessel was in 1859 to view the *Great Eastern* which was visiting the port. The second was in 1880 for the opening of the Railway Station! The only years in which regular services ran were 1883 (twice weekly), 1884 (three times a week) and 1888 when the ship left Douglas six evenings a week at 6.30 p.m. to connect with the Night Mail at Holyhead. The return departure was at 2.45 a.m.

A number of Steam Packet vessels have been chartered to run out of Holyhead for short periods on services to Ireland as recently as 1990. The *Victoria* was there in 1938 and *Mona's Isle* [5] and *Snaefell* [5] in the 1950s. In May

1978 the *Manxman* [2] called on a schools cruise. The *Mona's Queen* [5] saw service there in 1988 and the *Lady of Mann* [2] was there the following two years – during 1990 being chartered both to Sealink and B&I Line. With the size of vessels introduced at Holyhead in the opening years of the 21st century it would seem unlikely that any Steam Packet vessel would now be suitable even if one were available.

Before leaving Holyhead it should also be mentioned that, due to the threat of a seamen's strike which never materialised, the Isle of Man Government chartered the *Bolette* from Fred.Olsen to ensure that the 1988 TT races could still be run. She operated a small number of sailings from Holyhead to Douglas between 26th May and 12th June that year.

IRISH SERVICES

The first Steam Packet scheduled sailings to Belfast were not until April 1885 after the Whitehaven Steamship Co. withdrew the *Thistle*. There had previously been excursion sailings in 1848 and 1869 as well as a shareholder trip on the new *Snaefell* [1] in October 1863. Thereafter summer schedules have been operated except during wartime. Between the mid-1890s and the First World War there were services from Peel to Belfast with connecting trains to and from Douglas, but silting in Peel was a problem and between 1902 and 1908 all services ran from Douglas. Since the First World War there have been no regular Belfast sailings from Peel although there were two excursions in 1929. Peel was regularly used as a diversion port until the building of the Douglas breakwater in 1983. After the Second World War, Belfast services (from Douglas) resumed in 1947, although a Tynwald Day excursion in 1953 ran from Peel to Belfast.

Seasonal services on the Belfast route are now operated by fast craft, with extra tonnage being chartered on a voyage basis during the TT race period. In 2005 the extra sailings were operated from Larne to Douglas using the large Incat *P&O Express* which is based at that port. Steam Packet vessels have taken occasional charters out of Larne both to the Island and to the Clyde.

Moving south it is noted that *Tynwald* [3] was at Donaghadee on 14th August 1930, her last season of service with the Company, but there is no evidence that this was a regular port of call for the Company's vessels.

The Carlingford Lough ports of Greenore and Warrenpoint had a weekly service from Douglas most summers between 1877 and 1883 although in the early years only Greenore was served, with passengers for Warrenpoint being expected to transfer to a local steamer up the Lough. Such arrangements were less than satisfactory and from 1881 onwards all sailings covered both ports. There have been no scheduled sailings since 1883. When the *Manxman* [2] called at Warrenpoint in 1977 she was the first of the Company's vessels to visit the Lough since before the Second World War. When the

The **Mona's Isle** [5] *berthed at Belfast. (Ships of Mann collection)*

*The **Lady of Mann** [2] at Belfast. (Jenny Williamson)*

Lady of Mann [2] called at Greenore in 1980 she was the first passenger ship to visit the port for over forty years. She was there again two years later with a schools excursion, but only returned to the Lough to operate an excursion from Warrenpoint to Douglas in June 2000.

Regular summer Dublin services have operated for most of the Company's history – certainly from the mid-1840s onwards. The North British Railway also ran a year-round Silloth / Douglas / Dublin service up to 1890 so the Manx company by no means had a monopoly on the route. There was also competition between Kingstown (Dun Laoghaire) and Dublin to host Manx services and

both were used between 1898 and 1900. Kingstown had also been used as a destination for shareholder excursions by the *Tynwald* [1] in 1846, *Douglas* [2] in 1864 and *Tynwald* [2] in 1866. The *Queen Victoria* had also made two excursions there in 1889.

After the Second World War, regular services to Dublin did not resume until 1951, although there had been three excursions the previous year. In 1985 the *Mona's Isle* [6] unexpectedly took some Dublin sailings and had to be diverted to Dun Laoghaire to find a suitable linkspan, and in 1998 the *Tynwald* [6] used Dun Laoghaire for some autumn and winter sailings. Subsequently there have been October half-term and Christmas sailings between Dublin and Douglas.

In 1996 the *Lady of Mann* [2] operated a Fleetwood-Dublin service between 26th September and 28th October but this was never repeated, although the following year she re-opened the Liverpool-Dublin route, which was in 1998 taken over by a fast craft belonging to then parent company Sea Containers. The service reverted to the Steam Packet after Sea Containers sold out but was closed at the end of the 2004 season, only to be re-opened by a new company which chartered the withdrawn *SeaCat Isle of Man* (re-named *Sea Express 1*) for the service.

EVEN FURTHER AWAY FROM HOME

Three ships in the Company's peacetime history stand out for their capacity to earn revenue away from home:

The *Tynwald* [1] of 1846 ran on the Hull-Hamburg

*The **Lady of Mann** [2] turning to leave Douglas for the last time on Sunday 12th June 2005. (Miles Cowsill)*

*The **Lady of Mann** [2] on charter to Acor Line leaving Horta harbour on the island of Faial, one of a group of nine islands which make up the Azores, in September 2001. (Bryan Kennedy)*

services from Weymouth to the Channel Islands.

The record for by far the greatest time and mileage under charter – as well as distance from base - must however go to the *Lady of Mann* [2]. In 1995 she was chartered to Porto Santo Line to open a new service between Funchal (Madeira) and Porto Santo. In 1998 and 2000, and then each summer from 2002 to 2005, she has seen 90 days' service around the Azores with Acor Line where her side-loading capabilities have been ideal for operating from piers without linkspans. These charters undoubtedly contributed to the economics of keeping the 'Lady' a viable unit for TT and winter duties into her 30th year of Irish Sea service.

Perhaps the most fortuitous charter – in the sense of a ship being in the right place at the right time – was the *Mona's Queen* [5] in September 1989. She had sailed from Heysham to Cherbourg on 31st August for a short charter to La Poste in support of their entry at the start of a Round the World Yacht race. The Sealink ferry *Earl Granville* had hit some rocks and had to be withdrawn for repairs and so the *Mona's Queen* was immediately chartered for service on the Portsmouth-Cherbourg route (initially with her full Manx crew) until 14th September. Even then her luck held and she was switched to Weymouth until 23rd September, setting out for her 25-hour passage back to the Island the next morning.

route for three months in 1849 and was chartered for a 30-day voyage to Gibraltar, Genoa and Leghorn the following year. She did three spells of winter service on the Liverpool-Belfast route, in 1847/48 and again in 1852 and 1865.

The 1876-built *Snaefell* [2] was chartered for the first five months of 1877 to the Royal Netherlands Steamship Co. for service on their route between Queensborough and Flushing. In September 1890 she was on charter for several weeks to the Great Western Railway for their

*The **Moby Love,** formerly the **King Orry** (5), still retains very much her good looks from her time on the Irish sea and Dover Strait. (Bruce Peter)*

Towards the end of her time with the Steam Packet the **Lady of Mann** *(2) found charter work in the Azorian archipeligo. (Bryan Kennedy)*

LADY OF MANN
DOUGLAS

ΠΑΝΑΓΙΑ ΣΟΥΜΕΛΑ
ΠΕΙΡΑΙΑΣ   www.saos.gr SAOS FERRI

The **Lady of Mann** (2) was sold for further service to Greek operators SAOS Ferries and extensively altered around the stern to allow the carriage of commercial vehicles on their routes between the Greek Islands. Renamed **Panagia Soumela** she is seen here at the port of Agios Kirikos on the island of Ikaria in April 2008. (Bryan Kennedy)

CHAPTER SEVEN

Memorabilia

There is a surprising amount of Steam Packet memorabilia lying in the homes of many people on and off the Island who have had family who have worked at some time in their lives for the Company. Uniforms, caps, postcards, photographs, pieces of cutlery, china, silverware and an infinite amount of mementos from years of working on the vessels have been retained by families. From time to time disposal sales have also taken place and professional caterers have acquired silverware still in use today in local establishments.

In addition there is an even greater amount of material in the hands of museums, enthusiasts and collectors who have purchased bits and pieces from the scrap companies who have been breaking up the ships after their useful life has expired. Staircases, doors, brass signs, telegraphs, valves, crests, flags, toilets and the list goes on.

However, the ultimate accolade in memorabilia nearly went to the group of enthusiasts who tried to save a complete ship! They had hoped to acquire the *Manxman* [2] and restore her to something like her former glory and return her to Liverpool. Unfortunately the venture failed for lack of a berth on the Mersey but she was only broken-up as this book went to press in 2012.

Also included are a number of photographs of groups of crew members - kindly supplied by Ken Hassell - where it has not been possible to identify all the individuals. The publisher would be pleased to receive any information towards identifying them. I believe that the photographs were taken in the mid-1930s.

Thanks again to all those who afforded me access to their collections.

*Postcard collecting is a popular means of acquiring memorabilia of the Steam Packet ships. It is well illustrated here with this card showing Douglas Head lighthouse with the **Lady of Mann** (1) in white livery approaching Douglas from the south.*

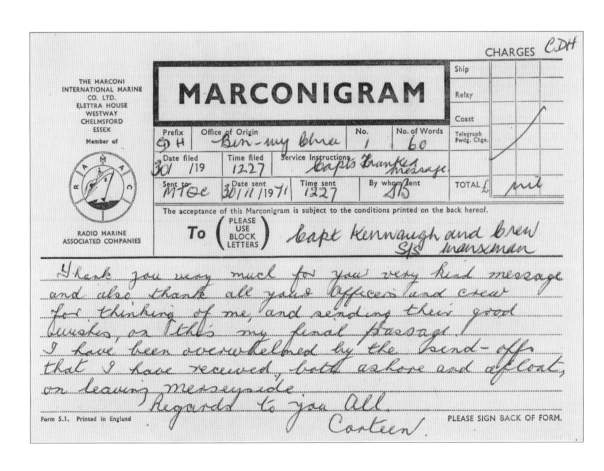

S-3
THE MARCONI INTERNATIONAL MARINE CO. LTD. ELETTRA HOUSE CHELMSFORD ESSEX

MARCONIGRAM

Prefix	Handed in at		No.	No. of Words	Date	Time	Service Instructions
CDH	Manxman		1	54	30/11/71	1150	

Date Received	Time Received	Received from	By
30/11/71	1205	MTGC SB	

TO

Capt T H Corteen S/S Ben-my-Chree
On behalf of the officers and crew Manxman
on the occasion of this your last trip in harness
our every good wish to yourself and Mrs Corteen
for a long and happy retirement good luck
and good health to enjoy and savour every
hard earned minute of it = Kennaugh Master

PTO

PRINTED IN ENGLAND

THE MARCONI
INTERNATIONAL MARINE
CO. LTD.
ELETTRA HOUSE
WESTWAY
CHELMSFORD
ESSEX

Member of

RADIO MARINE
ASSOCIATED COMPANIES

MARCONIGRAM

CHARGES CDH

Ship	
Relay	
Coast	
Telegraph Fwdg. Chge.	

Prefix	Office of Origin	No.	No. of Words
CDH	Ben-my-Chree	1	60

Date filed	Time filed	Service Instructions
30/ /19	1227	Capt's Transfer message

Sent to	Date sent	Time sent	By whom sent
MTGC	30/11/1971	1227	SB

TOTAL £ nil

The acceptance of this Marconigram is subject to the conditions printed on the back hereof.

To (PLEASE USE BLOCK LETTERS) Capt Kennaugh and Crew S/S Manxman

Thank you very much for your very kind message
and also thank all your officers and crew
for thinking of me, and sending their good
wishes, on this my final passage.
I have been overwhelmed by the kind-offs
that I have received, both ashore and afloat,
on leaving Merseyside.
Regards to you all.
Corteen.

Form S.1. Printed in England   PLEASE SIGN BACK OF FORM.

memorabilia

Top left , top right and middle right:
The traditional dining rooms of the Company vessels up to comparatively recent times were always silver-service. However, as times changed the Company found itself with a surfeit of silverware and from time to time offered it for sale. Much found its way into hotels and boarding houses and to private collectors. The elegant ware carried the insignia of the Steam Packet Company.

Right: *It was not only the Steam Packet that carried silverware - it was the order of the day. When the Steam Packet acquired their rival the Isle of Man, Liverpool & Manchester Steamship Co., also known as 'The Manx Line', they also acquired the silverware on their two vessels, the* **Prince of Wales** *and the* **Queen Victoria**. *This ware was in use into the 1980s often mixed with the Company's own. Here are two examples.*

THE VILLIERS HOTEL,

ISLE OF MAN.

HOTEL TARIFF.

Bedroom, including Attendance and Lights...from 2s 6d to 5s per night.
Breakfast . . . . . ,, 2s 0d
Luncheon . . . . . ,, 2s 0d
Dinner, to order . . . . ,, 2s 6d
Dinner (Table d'Hote) 3s 6d
Tea or Coffee, per Cup. . . . 6d

Full Table d'Hote Board, Bedroom, Attendance, and Lights, from 8s 6d to 10s 6d per Day, according to position of Bedroom.

When two visitors occupy the same bed a reduction of 1s per day is made.

Private Sitting Rooms, from 5s to 7s 6d per Day

ALL CHARGES IN THE HOTEL INCLUDE ATTENDANCE.

The Wine List will be found to comprise good, sound Wines, commencing at very moderate prices.

A portion of the Hotel is entirely set apart for the comfort and requirements of Commercial Gentlemen, who will receive every attention, upon the usual terms.

Reduced Terms for Winter Residence (for which the climate of the Isle of Man is peculiarly adapted), from October to March. Further particulars on application to the Manager.

An Illustrated Guide Book of the Island will be forwarded on receipt of Twelve Stamps.

4   Brown's Isle of Man Directory.

Liverpool & Douglas,

DAILY COMMUNICATION *(Sundays excepted)*.

LIVERPOOL TO AND FROM RAMSEY.
WHITEHAVEN TO AND FROM RAMSEY.
ISLE OF MAN TO AND FROM GLASGOW.

The Isle of Man Company's Royal Mail Steamship
Ben-my-Chree, King Orry, Snaefell, Tynwald, Douglas, Mona, Mona's
Isle, or Fenella (new steamer),

IS APPOINTED TO SAIL DAILY,

(Unless prevented by any unforeseen occurrence), leaving the PRINCE'S LANDING
STAGE, LIVERPOOL, Daily at 1 p.m., from the 1st of May to the end of September,
inclusive, and DOUGLAS at or after 9 Morning, except during July and August, when
on Mondays and Saturdays the Steamer will leave at 8 morning.
Goods received at North side of Queen's Half-tide Dock, and conveyed from Liverpool.
Communication is also Daily in Winter.   For hours of departure see Time Bills.

LIVERPOOL AND RAMSEY.

From LIVERPOOL every Monday | From RAMSEY every Saturday
See Sailing Bills.
SINGLE FARES.—To or from Liverpool and Douglas or Ramsey: Cabin, 6s; Steerage, 3s.   Half Fare under 12 years.   RETURN TICKETS: Cabin, 10s 6d; Steerage, 5s 6d.
These Tickets are available for Two Calendar Months, exclusive of the date of issue.

TOURIST TICKETS, available for Two Calendar Months, issued at the chief Stations
of the London and North-Western—Lancashire and Yorkshire—Great Western—Manchester, Sheffield, and Lincolnshire—Great Northern—North Stafford—Midland—
Cheshire Lines—and Manchester South Junction and Altrincham Railway Companies.

FLEETWOOD & DOUGLAS—Daily Service in the Season.

(Sundays excepted.)   Commencing about 25th June.   From DOUGLAS at 8 a.m.
From FLEETWOOD on arrival of Train due at 2 p.m.   Fares same as Liverpool.

WHITEHAVEN & RAMSEY—Every Fortnight.

See Sailing Bills.
SINGLE FARES: Cabin, 6s; Steerage, 3s.   RETURN TICKETS, available for a
Calendar Month, Cabin, 9s; Steerage, 4s 6d.   Return Tickets issued on the Whitehaven
Station are available *via* Liverpool on payment of the difference of fare.

ISLE OF MAN & CLYDE SERVICE—Weekly.

From Glasgow every Thursday.   From Douglas every Wednesday.
SINGLE FARES.—Cabin, 10s; Steerage, 5s.   RETURN TICKETS, available for Two
Months: Cabin, 15s; Steerage, 7s 6d.

ISLE OF MAN & IRELAND—Weekly.

For particulars see Time Bills.

For further information as to Fares, Luggage, &c., see Company's Time Bills.

AGENTS.

LIVERPOOL—THOMAS ORFORD & SON, 60, Tower Buildings South, Water-street.
WHITEHAVEN—GEORGE NELSON & SONS, Lowther-street.
MANCHESTER—T. COLES, 77A, Market-street.
GLASGOW—H. LAMONT, 93, Hope-street.
GREENOCK- W. LINDSAY & CO., East Quay.
RAMSEY—ROBERT H. TEARE, Steampacket Office.
FLEETWOOD—T. H. CARR.
DOUGLAS—THOMAS P. ELLISON.

*This is a fine study of the **Mona's Queen** [3] on 12th April 1934, the day of her launch from Cammell Laird's yard in Birkenhead. She is being taken to the fitting-out berth. It shows the size of the bow section which was the main point of controversy with those who commanded the vessel. The extra deck forward increased windage which made the vessel difficult to handle in harbour in storm conditions. (J & M Clarkson collection)*

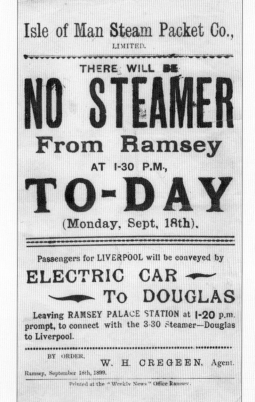

Four posters, reminders of the days when the Company operated as many as eight passenger vessels to cope with the peaks of weekend travel and offered special excursions to utilise vessels which otherwise would have been idle. Posters can also be a source of useful information and here we see that it is no new phenomenon with this charming poster advertising a Round the Island trip in 1927 (above) but going north about and picking up passengers from Ramsey. The Ramsey passengers are told that they will "return from Douglas by Steamer". What a tantalising snippet! How? Would it be on the Belfast or Ardrossan service? Which vessel would be used on the excursion? There are more questions than answers.

Such posters and notices tell us a lot about the society of the day and how information was broadcast. Here are more questions in this notice (left), printed on the day of sailing and presumably placed at strategic places around the town announcing the cancellation of the afternoon sailing to Liverpool, with passengers being conveyed by electric car (note the Manx Electric Railway even to this day do not refer to their cars as trams) to Douglas for the 3.30 p.m. steamer to Liverpool. So why? What was the problem that caused the cancellation? Was it a problem with the ship? Was it the weather? A visit to the Manx Museum and their reference library will provide the answer and I hope that someone will find it! That's called historical research and what many of us have enjoyed doing for many years - I hope it is encouraged by successive generations.

Memorabilia are described in my dictionary as "records of memorable events" and so this section of the 175 Album sets out to achieve just that. Enthusiasts collect all manner of memorabilia, as we shall see from photographs placed throughout this book, which without doubt stimulate the memory, from something small as a cap badge to a complete ship. Here are two montages of timetables and advertising brochures issued by the Company from which much historical information can be gleaned.

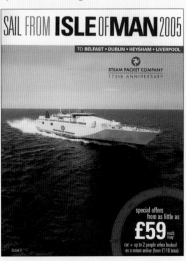

*The **Manx Maid** [1] was formerly the **Caesarea** of the London & South Western Railway Co. and was purchased by the Steam Packet Co. in December 1923. A triple-screw steamer, she is seen here before the Second World War at a so far unidentified location. (J & M Clarkson collection)*

Above: *We have seen the silverware already in this chapter and here it is fully laid out in the First Class dining room of the* **Mona's Queen** *[3] which is decorated in the wood veneer panelling typical of the 1930s. (Wirral Museum Service/Cammell Laird Archive)*

Left: *This photograph was taken on board the* **Lady of Mann** *[2] in 1980 and although the dining room is smaller and more spartan (remember what I wrote about photographs reflecting social change) the Steward is setting the silver service. (Stan Basnett)*

Right: *How ferry travel has changed over the years from silver service to cafeteria style operations in the light of high wage costs and less demand for quality food on the crossings to the Island. In 1989 the* **Lady of Mann** *underwent a major refit of her passenger areas. The top view shows the new cafeteria area and the view below the Cafe Express on B Deck. (Ferry Publications Library)*

memorabilia

It was originally intended that this book would encompass a detailed listing of the engineers employed by the Company and a separate chapter on the crew. Whilst the intention was good it has proved a daunting task way beyond the scope of this volume which has done no more than scratch the surface. It will be for others to pick up the tale and run with it.

Top and bottom left: *A considerable number of photographs of crew have come to light but it has proved almost impossible to identify them and in many cases the ship on which the photographs were taken. Any information on any of them would be happily received. (Ken Hassell collection)*

Bottom right: *Captain 'Ginger' Bridson is seen here on the **Viking** with on his right 'Pat' Stowell but with an as yet unidentified AB on his left. Anyone any idea who it may be? (Billy Stowell)*

Opposite page: *These are pages from Stowell's family's discharge books which need no explanation and make interesting reading. More importantly from the historical point of view, they contain a wealth of information on, for example, the Masters of certain vessels and when and where vessels were laid up. (Billy Stowell collection)*

CERTIFICATE OF DISCHARGE

E OF A SEAMAN NOT DISCHARGED BEFORE A SUPERINTENDENT OF A MERCANTILE MARINE OFFICE.

ISSUED BY THE BOARD OF TRADE IN PURSUANCE OF 57 & 58 VIC., CH. 60.

Name of Ship and Official Number, Port of Registry and Gross Tonnage.	Horse Power.	Description of Voyage or Employment.
Douglas Isle 120522. Douglas 1688		Home Trade

Name of Seaman.	Year of Birth.	Place of Birth.
J. W. Stowell	1897	Douglas IOM

Rank or Rating.	Numbers of Certificates (if any). Dis.A. No.	Any other Cert.
Fireman	—	—

Date of Engagement.	Place of Engagement.
31. 8. 34	Douglas I.O.M.

Date of Discharge.	Place of Discharge.
6. 9. 34	Douglas I.O.M.

I Certify that the above particulars are correct and that the above-named Seaman was discharged accordingly.

Dated this 6th day of September 193t

Signature of Master J Keig

Signature of Seaman:

Signature of Witness V E Clark

Occupation Mate

Address on board

NOTE.—Any person who forges or fraudulently alters any Certificate of Discharge, or who makes use of any such Certificate, which is forged or altered or does not belong to him, is guilty of a misdemeanour, and may be fined or imprisoned.

N.B.—Should this Certificate come into the possession of any person to whom it does not belong, it should be handed to the Superintendent of the nearest Mercantile Marine Office, or be transmitted to the Registrar General of Shipping and Seamen, Tower Hill, London, E.C. 3.

Price 4d. per quire.

*744. Wt. 10016/4311. 75M. 8/32. Wy.P.C. G.-613(8).

CERTIFICATE OF DISCHARGE

E OF A SEAMAN NOT DISCHARGED BEFORE A SUPERINTENDENT OF A MERCANTILE MARINE OFFICE.

ISSUED BY THE BOARD OF TRADE IN PURSUANCE OF 57 & 58 VIC., CH. 60.

Name of Ship and Official Number, Port of Registry and Gross Tonnage.	Horse Power.	Description of Voyage or Employment.
VIKING. 118604 DOUGLAS 1956	1100	COAST WISE

Name of Seaman.	Year of Birth.	Place of Birth.
J. W. STOWELL	1897	DOUGLAS I.O.M.

Rank or Rating.	Numbers of Certificates (if any). Dis.A. No.	Any other Cert.
FIREMAN		CL 65L76

Date of Engagement.	Place of Engagement.
16 MAY 1934	Barrow-in-Furness

Date of Discharge.	Place of Discharge.
18/8/34	Douglas

I Certify that the above particulars are correct and that the above-named Seaman was discharged accordingly.

Dated this 18th day of August 1934

Signature of Master W Watson

Signature of Seaman:

Signature of Witness S Cain

Occupation Purser

Address VIKING

NOTE.—Any person who forges or fraudulently alters any Certificate of Discharge, or who makes use of any such Certificate, which is forged or altered or does not belong to him, is guilty of a misdemeanour, and may be fined or imprisoned.

N.B.—Should this Certificate come into the possession of any person to whom it does not belong, it should be handed to the Superintendent of the nearest Mercantile Marine Office, or be transmitted to the Registrar General of Shipping and Seamen, Tower Hill, London, E.C. 3.

Price 4d. per quire.

*744. Wt. 10016/4311. 75M. 8/32. Wy.P.C. Gp. 613(8).

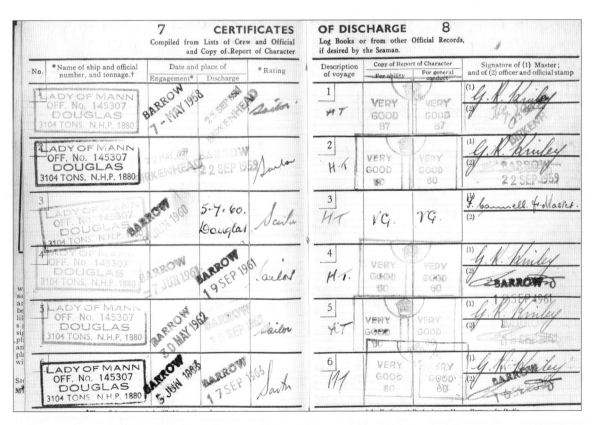

No.	*Name of ship and official number, and tonnage.†	Date and place of Engagement*	Discharge	*Rating	Description of voyage	Copy of Report of Character — For ability	For general conduct	Signature of (1) Master; and of (2) officer and official stamp
1	LADY OF MANN OFF. No. 145307 DOUGLAS 3104 TONS. N.H.P. 1880	BARROW 7 - MAY 1958	23 SEP 1958 BIRKENHEAD	Sailor	1 HT	VERY GOOD 87	VERY GOOD 87	(1) G. K. Kinley (2)
2	LADY OF MANN OFF. No. 145307 DOUGLAS 3104 TONS. N.H.P. 1880	30 MAY 1959 BIRKENHEAD	BARROW 22 SEP 1959	Sailor	2 H.T	VERY GOOD 80	VERY GOOD 80	(1) G. K. Kinley (2) BARROW 22 SEP 1959
3	LADY OF MANN OFF. No. 145307 DOUGLAS 3104 TONS. N.H.P. 1880	BARROW 7 JUN 1960	5. 7. 60. Douglas	Sailor	3 HT	VG.	VG.	(1) T. Cannell Jr Master (2)
4	LADY OF MANN OFF. No. 145307 DOUGLAS 3104 TONS. N.H.P. 1880	BARROW 27 JUN 1961	BARROW 19 SEP 1961	Sailor	4 HT.	VERY GOOD 80	VERY GOOD 80	(1) G. K. Kinley (2) BARROW 19 SEP 1961
5	LADY OF MANN OFF. No. 145307 DOUGLAS 3104 TONS. N.H.P. 1880	BARROW 30 MAY 1962	BARROW 18 SEP 1962	Sailor	5 HT	VERY GOOD	VERY GOOD	(1) G. K. Kinley (2)
6	LADY OF MANN OFF. No. 145307 DOUGLAS 3104 TONS. N.H.P. 1880	BARROW 5 JUN 1963	BARROW 17 SEP 1963	South	6 HT	VERY GOOD 80	VERY GOOD 80	(1) G. K. Kinley (2) BARROW

7   CERTIFICATES   OF DISCHARGE   8

Compiled from Lists of Crew and Official and Copy of Report of Character

Log Books or from other Official Records, if desired by the Seaman.

Top: *The **Manxman** [2] prior to leaving Douglas for the last time in September 1982. (Stan Basnett)*

Below: *The **Manxman** as she was in 2005, after a somewhat chequered career, sitting forlorn in Pallion dry dock in Sunderland. The Manxman Steamship Co. Ltd was formed by a group of enthusiasts whose aim is to restore her to her former glory and bring her back to Liverpool to become part of the maritime collection. Unfortunately the venture failed for lack of a berth on the Mersey but she was only being broken up as this book went to press in 2012. (Adrian Sweeney/Ships of Mann)*

ISLE OF MAN

HEALTH – PLEASURE – SUNSHINE

TURBINE STEAMERS "BEN-MY-CHREE" & "VIKING".
ISLE OF MAN STEAM PACKET Cº LTD.
(Incorporated in the Isle of Man)

GREAT CENTRAL RAILWAY

EXPRESS SERVICE TO THE ISLE OF MAN
Via LIVERPOOL (3¼ HOURS SEA PASSAGE)

By Express Turbine Royal Mail Steamer "BEN-MY-CHREE" (25 Knots).

FOR PARTICULARS OF
Train Service, Excursion and Tourist Tickets,
SEE GREAT CENTRAL TIME TABLES, BILLS AND PROGRAMMES.

Passengers, their luggage, live stock and goods conveyed subject only to the conditions of carriage of the Company as exhibited in their offices and on board their steamers.

*I never imagined that this double spread of the **Ben-my-Chree** [5] arriving at Douglas on the tail of an easterly gale would be considered as being of historical interest some day. It was taken from the head of the Battery Pier in January 1968 proving the old adage that "today's news is tomorrow's history". (Stan Basnett)*

CHAPTER EIGHT

Into the Future

As we have seen in the last chapter, memorabilia is all about the past and nostalgia. We must remember that the Steam Packet is not living in the past but very much of the moment and still providing an essential lifeline between the Isle of Man and the UK. In fact its winter service is providing twice the number of daily sailings that have existed since the Second World War. What then of the future?

This second edition of **Steam Packet 175 the Album** has been published in 2012 in response to demand some seven years on from 2005. The opportunity has been taken therefore to provide some additional text and photographs and to give a short review of what has happened since. The Company has always been at the forefront of development when it has come to the choice of vessel to use on their Irish Sea routes. At the outset it was one of the first companies to use a steam paddle ship on the Irish Sea. The *Mona's Isle* had an overall length of 33.3m and a gross tonnage of 200 tons, its side lever engine (a derivative of the beam engine) had a nominal rating of 100 hp and a service speed of 8 knots.

The ultimate development of the paddle steamer came in 1897 with the introduction of the *Empress Queen* considered to be the best steam paddle ship in the British Isles. She was 113.38 long overall, her compound engines, rated at 10,000 hp, gave her a service speed of 21½ knots and she could carry 1,994 passengers. This was achieved at considerable cost when we consider that sixteen firemen were required to stoke her thirty-two boilers. The Company was without doubt the leading shipping company of its day.

But there were to be no more paddle steamers, the Company had introduced its first single screw steamer in 1878. When the *Mona* [2] joined the fleet she was shorter and slower than the *Empress Queen*. She was introduced principally for the winter service and was the first passenger and cargo vessel. The advantage of the screw and economy both in space and fuel consumption of its vertical compound engine were soon seen.

Steam screw driven vessels incorporating single, twin and triple screws were incorporated into subsequent ships to keep ahead of the competition which came mainly from

*The **Ben-my-Chree** (6) arrives at Douglas on her afternoon sailing from Heysham with the **Snaefell** (6) at the Victoria Pier berth during her last season with the company. (Miles Cowsill)*

*The **Viking** (2) arrives from Liverpool at Douglas sporting the new Steam Packet livery. The Italian-built craft very much suited the new black hull livery introduced by the company in 2005. (Miles Cowsill)*

the railway steamers. Once again the Company became a trend setter with the introduction of the triple screw *Viking 1* in 1905. Three years later they introduced *Ben-my-Chree* (3) which was larger and incorporated lessons learned from the *Viking* and she became the flagship of the fleet.

She was 118.56m long overall and was the longest vessel owned by the Company until the introduction of *Ben-my-Chree* [6] in 1998 and she could carry 2,549 passengers with a crew of 119. The three turbine engines developed 14,000hp and gave her a speed of 24½ knots. She held the record for the Douglas to Liverpool Bar at 2hrs 23mins which was only beaten by the introduction of the fast craft almost a hundred years later. With a fuel consumption of 95 tons of coal per day and 22 firemen to stoke the boilers such speed was only achieved at considerable cost.

The Company lost seven ships altogether from its involvement in the First World War and took some time to recover. At one time consideration was given to liquidating the Company but a brave decision was made and it survived. It took a decade for it to recover.

Arguably the ultimate development of the traditional cross channel steamer came in the form of the centenary steamer *Lady of Mann* [1]. Introduced in 1930 she was a twin screw geared, turbine driven, oil fired vessel with an overall length of 113.08m and a service speed of 22 knots on a shaft indicated horse power of 12,700. She often exceeded her design speed in service and more so when on Government service during the Second World War. Along with her two slightly smaller consorts *Ben-my-Chree* [4]

and *Mona's Queen* [4] they were recognised as the finest ships of their type.

The last of the conventional passenger ships was the *Manxman* [2] designed to carry 2,393 passengers with 68 crew she had a service speed of 21 knots. Her claim to fame was that she was fitted with revolutionary Pametrada double reduction turbines fed by superheated steam. It was unfortunately too late but it did pave the way for the two steam driven car ferries and good use of the compact power plant enabled the machinery space to be accommodated comfortably below the car deck.

The Company was slow to provide a ro-ro service and came in for much criticism at the time by the public and the travel industry who were perhaps not aware of the circumstances that mitigated against its introduction. In the 1960s all of the ports served by the Company didn't have ro-ro facilities and most also had restrictions on available draft. Douglas in addition was limited by the space available for berthing and swinging a vessel. Peel was the diversionary port for Douglas which was untenable in easterly gales and it too had restrictions on available draft at all states of the tide.

There was another consideration which made the company hesitant to expend capital on such a venture. It was that the convention of carrying freight by road trailers across a stretch of water pre-supposed an onward journey reducing dock handling time. The Isle of Man was perceived as not viable in this regard and they saw no reason to change their existing freight handling method as cars and small vans were being conveyed on their side-loading car ferries. It should also be remembered that the Vehicle Construction and Use Regulations on the Island restricted the maximum length and weight of commercial vehicles below that of the rest of the UK. It was not long since visiting vehicles to the Island had to carry an island road fund tax disc which were issued on the pier by officials of the IoM Highway Board Licensing Department!

The Island's government was not prepared to spend money on harbour improvements so it was not surprising that the Company opted for side-loading car ferries. The first two were steam driven and the latter two were their first passenger motor vessels. The first motor-driven car ferry was the *Mona's Queen* [5] she was a twin-screw vessel powered by two 10 cylinder PC2 Crossley Pielstick engines producing 10,000 hp and giving a service speed of 21 knots. The second motor vessel was *Lady of Mann* [2] and she was similar in every respect except that her engines were V 12s producing 11,500 hp giving a service speed of 22 knots.

Although they were considered to be old technology compared with other car ferries they served the company and the Island well. The steam bow thrust units retro fitted to the two earlier car ferries even aroused the interest of the Royal Navy. The *Lady of Mann* (2) did see some charter work in Madeira and the Azorean archipelago as we have seen in the Away from Home chapter where no ro-ro facilities existed at the ports served.

Competition and a changed political environment in the Island favouring a competitor in the form of Manx Line forced the Company's hand and they were forced into the ro-ro business using second hand tonnage. They had restrictions imposed on the type of linkspan they could use which again disadvantaged their operation. It could be reasonably argued that their linkspan was side loading! It had also to be capable of being repositioned as the harbour was redeveloped.

The subsequent history of the Company, its merger with Manx Line and becoming part of the Sealink operation is covered elsewhere. Suffice to say that it eventually became privately owned and tied to an international finance provider. There were initially many advantages to this phase of the Company's history and we saw a huge and significant investment in a new ship *Ben-my-Chree* [6] which was the first purpose built ro-pax ship built by the Company. She remains the largest vessel they have owned and with a length of 125m overall and a gross tonnage of 12,504 she is also the longest.

She is without doubt the longest ship to use Douglas at all states of the tide and is not far off the largest that could use the port without there being extensive alterations to the outer harbour. Although coming from a standard design she was modified to fit the port restrictions which in a way still plague the Company. Nonetheless it has met all the requirements for serving the Company and the Island reliably and economically. With a capacity for 275 vehicles, 666 passengers and a freight lane length availability of 1,235m and two return sailings every twenty-four hours it continues to provide an all year round service well. That equates to 1½ miles of commercial vehicles every day.

*The company now heads into the future with two vessels, **Ben-my-Chree** (6) and **Manannan**. The 'Ben', which has proved exceptionally reliable and proved that it is more than capable of serving the Island's needs, is seen here turning onto the Edward Pier linkspan. (Miles Cowsill)*

*Throughout its existence the Company has had to fight off competition. The latest in 2010 was a Lift-On Lift-Off freight service operated by Mezeron/Dohle. The **Ingeborg Pilot** was one of the chartered vessels used on the short-lived service. (Stan Basnett)*

With its close ties to Sealink and Hoverspeed the Island, as we have seen already, gained valuable experience with the use of high speed craft on the Irish Sea routes. They proved extremely popular with the travelling public because of the shorter journey times but as we have seen in this review speed always comes with a cost and full loadings are essential to make such a venture possible.

The Company continued to operate fast craft up to 2005 using various craft on charter. In that year *Seacat Isle of Man* and *Superseacat Two* operated the summer service. At the end of that year *Seacat Isle of Man* was withdrawn by the Company and chartered to Irish Sea Express operating as *Sea Express 1*. Also in 2005 *Lady of Mann* [2] was withdrawn after completing her summer charter in the Azores and offered for sale. She was purchased in October 2005 by SAOS Ferries for operation in Greek waters. For the following year *Sea Express 1* was sub chartered back to the company as a consort to *Superseacat Two* with *Ben-my-Chree* [6] maintaining the core Heysham route, and peak traffic supplemented by charter vessels as required.

On 3rd February 2007 *Sea Express 1* operating Steam Packet sailings was involved in a collision with *Alaska Rainbow* in the Mersey in dense fog sustaining hull damage which required substantial repair work. It re-entered service with the Company in March 2008 in new Steam Packet colours and carrying the name *Snaefell* [6]. The new colours had also been applied to *Superseacat Two* which had been renamed *Viking* [2] and the mew colour scheme suited the fast craft exceptionally well.

The need for a new catamaran wave piercing craft had been under consideration for some time and in 2008 the Company purchased hull 050 from Incat Tasmania. After an extensive refit following a five-year charter to the US armed forces she entered service on 11th May 2009 as *Manannan* becoming the largest fast craft to operate on the Irish Sea routes with a service speed of 35 knots and a maximum of 40. Such speed as we have seen through the history of the Company comes at a cost and *Manannan* is no exception. She soon, however, found favour with the travelling public with her much shorter crossing times.

She is powered by four Caterpillar 3618 marine diesel engines giving a propulsion power of 28,800 Kw equivalent to 36,621 hp. She is 96m long overall and can carry 850 passengers with 200 vehicles. With the *Viking* [2] now surplus to requirements she was sold in September to Hellenic Lines after completing her summer charter.

In June 2010, fortunately after the peak TT traffic *Manannan* suffered a crankshaft failure in one of her 3618 Caterpillar engines resulting in the craft running at reduced speed on three engines for the rest of the season. Incredibly *Snaefell* [6] suffered a similar problem shortly after and she too continued on reduced power.

The Company had struggled with the machinations of finance and the subsequent sale to a financial institution saw the income was struggling to service the debt and leaving little profit to fund significant future expansion.

We have seen that Mr Sherwood acquired a controlling interest in the Steam Packet in 1996 after which it became a private company. We have also seen how its links with Sealink and Hoverspeed saw the introduction of fast craft

The 98m InCat 050 as Top Cat of Fast Cat Ferries Ltd in dry dock to await conversion for military operation as HSV-X1 **Joint Venture**. *(IoM Steam Packet)*

on the Isle of Man routes which placed the company back in its pioneering role.

In October 2005 the Macquarie Investment Bank purchased the Steam Packet but the following year in October sold 90% of its shareholding to three Australian Pension Funds retaining 10% as a management arm of the business.

A competitor for the freight business came in the form of a Lift on-Lift off daily service operating between Douglas and Liverpool which commenced in October 2010. It was operated by a local company Mezeron who for a number of years had operated a similar service from Ramsey to Glasson Dock and Northern Ireland. This expanded service was achieved through a partnership with Döhle (IOM) Ltd and employed Estonian registered ships on the service.

This was in response to a dispute that the Island's freight operators had with the Steam Packet over freight charges. Very quickly its effect was being felt by the Steam Packet and they lost number of their major freight clients to the competition. The dispute became acrimonious with the Island's Government and Unions becoming involved. The Government was called upon to nationalise the Steam Packet but such a move was defeated when put to the vote in December.

The matter was resolved quite suddenly in January 2011 when Mezeron announced that their service would cease by the middle of the month. The reason given was that the service did not generate sufficient business to meet

HSV-X1 **Joint Venture** *on evaluation with US forces during which time she saw service in the Persian Gulf. (InCat)*

InCat 050 pictured at Portsmouth in the early stages of her conversion. (IoM Steam Packet)

After the Company purchased InCat 050, it was taken to Portsmouth in 2008 where Burgess Marine undertook a major refit to make the vessel suitable for commercial Ro-Pax traffic. The pictures show the removal of the flight deck to provide additional accommodation aft and work in progress on the forward passenger lounge. (IoM Steam Packet)

their projected targets. The company continued their Ramsey-based service using their coaster *Silver River*. There followed an uneasy period with the Island's Government awaiting reports from the Office of Fair Trading into the fare structure of the Steam Packet with a possible further review of the User Agreement being considered.

Then on 8th April 2011 the Steam Packet announced that the share capital of the company previously owned by the Australian pension funds and Macquarie had been transferred to Sealion (Isle of Man) Ltd, a company owned by the IoM Steam Packet Company's banks led by Banco Espirito Santo. Following the refinancing of the business a new corporate structure was put in place. The Company was now in a much better place to move forward as master of its own destiny once again.

The fleet from the start of 2011 consisted of just two vessels the *Ben-my-Chree* [6] and the wave piercing craft *Manannan*. With its service now dependent on just two vessels its reliability was to be put to the test. Many people on the Island were concerned that it would ask too much to depend on 100% reliability and effectively have just one vessel for its all year round service.

Unfortunately this was to be put to the test sooner than expected when the *Ben-my-Chree* [6] ingested debris into one of her bow thrust units damaging it beyond repair. Fortunately throughout the summer period she was able to maintain her summer schedule. To add to the Company's problems *Manannan* suffered a a catastrophic failure of one of the gearboxes driving an impeller and had to operate for most of the season on reduced power until late in the

into the future

Work in progress extending the accommodation aft to provide lounges, bar facilities, toilets and ancillary accommodation. The four water propulsion jets are clearly visible in this dry dock photograph. (IoM Steam Packet)

season when repair was effected at Douglas during an early spell of bad weather.

During the last quarter of the year the weather in the Irish Sea continued with gales from the west and south west causing cancellations of sailings due in part to the problems with the *Ben-my-Chree* [6] still having only one

bow thrust unit working and the exposed conditions at Heysham harbour.

In December the replacement bow thrust unit was delivered and the 'Ben' dry docked at Birkenhead for it to be fitted. It couldn't have been a worse time for the Company on the run up to Christmas and adverse weather

Now afloat and final fitting out taking place. (IoM Steam Packet)

*InCat 050, now renamed **Manannan** and painted out in the latest Steam Packet livery, prepares to leave Portsmouth for the Isle of Man and her homeport of Douglas. (IoM Steam Packet)*

*The **Ben-my-Chree** (6) arriving at Douglas during the TT Races in May 2012.*
(Miles Cowsill)

*The **Manannan** arriving at Douglas on Tuesday 20h April 2010 with the fastcraft **Snaefell** (6) in the background berthed at No. 3 berth on the Victoria Pier. (Stan Basnett)*

continuing to cause delays to sailings. The *Manannan* was brought into service to cover the period of dry-docking and maintained the schedule in spite of the weather including a return Dublin/Isle of Man sailing.

At the start of 2012 the north west of England experienced some extreme weather that affected all transport systems throughout the region, which included Heysham harbour and its approaches leading to further

cancellations. However, the *Ben-my-Chree* [6], back to full power for her manoeuvrability, did manage to use narrow windows of opportunity to get in some sailings.

So the Company is set to continue with just two vessels and as it enters the next stage in its history there remains a balance between maintaining a profitable business and a service to the Island.

*The **Manannan** leaving Douglas on her scheduled departure on 25th April 2012 to Liverpool in a strong north-easterly blow where she showed her good sea keeping qualities once clear of the harbour mouth, arriving at Liverpool on time. (Stan Basnett)*

*During the 2012 **Ben-my-Chree** (6) refit period all freight traffic between Heysham and Douglas was handled by the chartered NorthLink freighter **Helliar**. She is being assisted by Laxey Towing Co.'s **Wendy Ann** as turning in Douglas outer harbour is always difficult in any north-easterly wind. (Stan Basnett)*

12/10/12 W3